SHIFT

SHIFT

Inside Nissan's Historic Revival

CARLOS GHOSN

AND PHILIPPE RIÈS

Translated from the French by John Cullen

CURRENCY

DOUBLEDAY

NEW YORK · LONDON · TORONTO · SYDNEY · AUCKLAND

A CURRENCY BOOK
PUBLISHED BY DOUBLEDAY
a division of Random House, Inc.

CURRENCY is a trademark of Random House, Inc., and DOUBLEDAY is a
registered trademark of Random House, Inc.

Cataloging-in-Publication Data is on file with the Library of Congress.
ISBN: 0-385-51290-2
All Rights Reserved

Book design by Fearn Cutler de Vicq
PRINTED IN THE UNITED STATES OF AMERICA

This book was originally published in France as *Citoyen du monde* by Carlos Ghosn and
Philippe Riès in 2003 by Bernard Grasset. © Éditions Grasset & Fasquelle, 2003.

First US Edition: © January 2005. Translated from the French by John Cullen.

All trademarks are the property of their respective companies.

SPECIAL SALES
Currency Books are available at special discounts for bulk purchases for sales
promotions or premiums. Special editions, including personalized covers, excerpts of existing
books, and corporate imprints, can be created in large quantities for special needs. For more
information, write to Special Markets, Currency Books,
specialmarkets@randomhouse.com.
1 3 5 7 9 10 8 6 4 2

CONTENTS

PREFACE

by

Philippe Riès

In the heart of the central business district in Tokyo stands Japanese industry's Holy of Holies, the Keidanren Kaikan. This building houses one of the most powerful business organizations on the planet. Japan's corporations, together with the state bureaucracy and the conservative politicians of the Liberal Democratic Party (LDP), form an "iron triangle" that has governed the country since the end of the American occupation at the beginning of the 1950s.

An unusual event took place in the vast auditorium of the Keidanren Kaikan on March 27, 1999, one that was rendered even more extraordinary by the setting itself. The event was an announcement: A foreign white knight had arrived to rescue a jewel in the crown of Japanese industrial enterprise, Nissan Motor Company, Ltd. Nissan was the number-two firm in the Japanese automobile industry, which itself was the second-largest in the world next to the United States. Despite its woes, Nissan Motor remained an industrial giant, with 140,000 salaried employees and, counting its *keiretsu* connections and its suppliers, close to half a million dependents. Its economic weight was greater than 1% of the country's gross domestic product. It was a global enterprise, with factories in the United States, Mexico, Europe, and Asia, and industrial or commercial networks spread across five continents. And, finally, it was a brand name known from Alaska to Tierra del Fuego, from the North Cape to the

Cape of Good Hope, one of those names that had helped the Japanese industrial machine penetrate the everyday consciousness of the peoples of the world. "Nissan" is a contraction of the words *nihon sangyō*, whose literal meaning is "Japanese industry"; the company has been an important part of Japanese history and shares many intimate traits of Japan's national character.

The date of March 27 had not been picked at random. Four days later, on March 31, 1999, Japanese companies would close their books on fiscal year 1998, which had begun the previous April. For Nissan, it had been another period of heavy losses, the seventh in eight years.

Nearly fifteen years earlier, in his book *The Reckoning*, David Halberstam had celebrated Nissan as the company that best represented the modern-day samurais who had dared to challenge Detroit on its own ground. Now, after a steady, twenty-six-year decline in its share of the Japanese automotive market, the firm was buckling under an enormous burden of debt and teetering on the verge of bankruptcy. Barring an unlikely intervention by the Japanese government, Nissan faced a simple choice: either enter voluntary liquidation or beseech a savior from abroad. After many long months of deliberation, and with the March 31, 1999, deadline looming, Nissan's management chose the latter solution. But it was not until the last moment that the name of the foreign partner emerged, and that name was, to say the least, a surprise.

DAVID AND GOLIATH

For a long time, Renault had been the ugly duckling of the automotive world. Recently privatized, the company was still dependent on the French government, which was by far its largest stockholder. Outside of France, the name Renault evoked nothing so much as a series of setbacks. Renault's small sedan, the Dauphine, had achieved limited success in America, but no similar successes followed. Instead, there had been a fiasco: the purchase of AMC, the American Motor Corporation, subsequently resold to Chrysler after devouring billions of francs. More recently, the collapse of a planned merger with Volvo Car had seemed to seal the fate of a company shackled by its past as a state-owned concern, excessively dependent on its domestic market, and almost certainly doomed to lose its independent status in the mighty process of consolidation that was about to reconfigure the worldwide automotive industry. Accordingly, the favorite to take over control of Nissan was the new giant of the automotive industry, the product of an audacious merger between Daimler-Benz AG and Chrysler Motor Corporation.

Having gobbled up one of Detroit's Big Three (albeit the smallest one, with the most troubled history), Jürgen Schrempp, the CEO of DaimlerChrysler, was turning his gaze to Asia. On paper, the contest between Renault SA and DaimlerChrysler AG to win the hearts of the directors of Nissan looked very much like David and Goliath. As quoted on the stock exchanges of Frankfurt and New York, the German-American outfit was roughly ten times richer than its French competitor. For the Japanese executives, if they were going to lose their independence, it was probably easier psychologically to sell their company to Germans. After all, Mercedes, BMWs, Audis, and Volkswagens had such strong appeal for Japanese consumers that Germany was the only country whose automotive trade with Japan was in balance. German-made automobiles represented a good two-thirds of the vehicles imported by Japan. Renault had sold fewer than 3,000 units in Japan in 1998. And finally, DaimlerChrysler, whose Mercedes and Freightliner models made it the number-one truck manufacturer in the world, could excite the Nissan directors with the prospect of saving Nissan Diesel, a truck-manufacturing subsidiary in even worse shape than its corporate parent.

But the French were able to find some advantages in their small size and relative poverty. The decision to contact Nissan was the result of careful deliberation. After the painful failure of an attempted merger with Volvo, Louis Schweitzer, Renault's chairman and CEO, realized that he had to look to other frontiers as rapidly as possible.

THE CRISIS OF "JAPAN INC."

Behind its uniform appearance, the Japanese automotive industry was in reality marked by sharp contrasts. Toyota had climbed into third place worldwide, and in the course of its rise to prominence, the company had received virtually universal acclaim for its production system, "the machine that changed the world." From its headquarters in Nagoya, Toyota now controlled more than 40% of the Japanese market and was extending its reach across the planet, thanks in part to its formidable financial clout. Honda Motor was also in excellent shape and well on the way to becoming Japan's second-largest automobile manufacturer. Honda's strength lay in its engineering; its design innovations had attracted young consumers and transformed Honda's U.S. operation into a bastion of profitability. Sure of itself and confident in its future, Honda was a fiercely, resolutely independent company. But the other Japanese car manufacturers were experiencing the pain associated with what came to be known in Japan as the "lost decade." It had begun in 1990, following the bursting of the Japanese stock market bubble created in the 1980s, and it caused widespread financial pain and crippling uncertainty. Mazda was now effectively under American control through its affiliation with Ford. Companies of even more modest size—Isuzu, Fuji Heavy (maker of Subaru), and Suzuki—had sought protection under the wing of General Motors, the largest automotive manufacturer in the world. The only independent manufacturers remaining were Mitsubishi Motor Corporation (MMC) and Nissan.

In all likelihood, Nissan's fate had been sealed in the fall of 1997, in the midst of a financial panic, when the president of Fuji Bank indicated that he had no intention of flying to the rescue of a securities firm, Yamaichi Securities, even though it was a member of the *keiretsu* that the Fuyo group had built around the bank. Nissan also belonged to this group. Although it was certainly less homogeneous than the Mitsubishi, Mitsui, or Sumitomo conglomerates, the companies that constituted the Fuyo *keiretsu* nevertheless shared a common history and reciprocal obligations. The bankruptcy of Yamaichi Securities, one of the four largest Japanese brokerage houses, combined with the ensuing failure of the Takugin Bank, revealed with unequivocal clarity how advanced the erosion of the entire Japanese financial system was. The relative underdevelopment of Japan's capital markets meant that its companies were nearly completely dependent on bank financing. Now, in exchange for a partial recapitalization using public funds, a law passed in the aftermath of the 1997–1998 financial crisis, Japanese banks were called upon to tidy up their balance sheets. Historically, Nissan had been able to count on the support of two great banks: Fuji, a commercial bank, and—to a greater extent— IBJ (Industrial Bank of Japan), the biggest of the three long-term credit banks that had played a key role in the reconstruction and expansion of the Japanese economy. IBJ's ties to Nissan were tight and complex; over the years, the bank had furnished the company not only with "the sinews of war" but also with a number of generals—bank executives who were assigned to important posts in the Nissan hierarchy to guide the firm through difficult times. Such assignments had been standard practice during Japan's period of economic growth, but now IBJ was in deep trouble. However, unlike its two chief rivals, LTCB (Long Term Credit Bank of Japan) and NCB (Nippon Credit Bank), IBJ would be able to escape (barely) failure and nationalization; it would owe its survival solely to the merger process that eventually established the Mizuho Financial Group. Early in 1999, a good part of this history remained to be written, but for the directors of Nissan, the conclusion was already implicit: The company would have to find another road to safety.

Could the Japanese government help? Nationalization is not common in Japan, where the influence of the state upon economic life, though pervasive, runs through different channels, principally its powerful bureaucracy. A failing bank had small hope of being rescued by an infusion of taxpayers' money; in the case of an industrial firm, there was no hope at all.

Could Nissan receive a helping hand from one of its Japanese rivals? The Japanese automotive industry, like its counterparts in the other industrialized nations, had indeed experienced some internal reshuffling. In the 1960s, Nissan itself had absorbed Prince Motor. Toyota was asserting more and more control over Daihatsu, the mini-car manufacturer, and had moreover purchased the heavy-vehicle manufacturer Hino. Despite this history, however, the answer to the question was evident: a categorical "No." There were, in fact, only two possibilities, Toyota and Honda. Could Nissan and Honda, ranked second and third among Japan's automobile manufacturers, join together? It would be like a rabbit marrying a trout, two entirely different animals. As for Toyota, such a merger would be tantamount to asking Nissan's 140,000 employees to give up. During the previous decades, Nissan's obsession with overtaking Toyota had turned to bitterness as its goal receded farther and farther into the distance. Its obstinate pursuit of Toyota had played a major role in leading Nissan astray, as it became more concerned with imitating its chief rival than with developing its own personality.

Necessity forced Nissan to look for a foreign partner.

A PERFECT FIT

When the Daimler-Chrysler merger took place, Renault, small and exclusively European, was financially and commercially weakened. Analysts at the time estimated that an annual production of 4 million vehicles would mark the threshold of survival for major automotive manufacturers. Renault's production was far below this figure. Admittedly, the firm's capital remained in a lockbox because of the significant (44.4%) residual participation of the French government. But this was a Maginot Line, a defensive position that could be undermined at any moment. The French government no longer considered itself called upon to act as a shareholder in commercial enterprises. If Renault was to remain in control of its destiny, it had to grow, and grow fast.

The studies carried out by Renault's international team quickly came to two conclusions: The road to the future passed through Asia, and the ideal partner in Asia was Nissan. On a geographical level, the fit was nearly perfect. Renault was very powerful in Europe, where Nissan, despite an excellent manufacturing plant in Sunderland, on the northeast coast of England, enjoyed only a modest share of the European market, a share similar to that of the other Japanese carmakers. On the other hand, Nissan was well established in Japan and Asia, where Renault's presence was minimal. Renault was making great strides in South America, while Nissan had a presence in Mexico. Finally, Nissan was selling more than 700,000 vehicles annually in the United States, from which Renault had withdrawn ingloriously after the failure of its AMC acquisition.

An examination of the capabilities and strengths of the two companies reveals an equally high degree of synergy. Nissan's engineering was still world-class, particularly their engines and transmissions, and as with most Japanese companies, Nissan was a leader in production systems and quality control. Renault excelled in areas where the Japanese manufacturer was weak: conceptual innovation, original design, purchasing, marketing, brand identity, and financial expertise.

COURTING NISSAN

Of Nissan's three potential suitors, Renault was the least powerful, the least financially well off, and the least prestigious. Yoshikazu Hanawa, Nissan's president, flirted hard first with DaimlerChrysler (initially approached to rescue the company's truck affiliate, Nissan

Diesel), and then Ford. But Ford's control of Mazda already gave it a production base in Japan and Asia, and besides, the number-two American automotive manufacturer was already in the process of completing or digesting important acquisitions in Europe, most notably Volvo Car. Jac Nasser, Ford's CEO, while not totally rejecting Hanawa, displayed little enthusiasm for the union. For its part, DaimlerChrysler had placed the bar very high: It demanded a majority interest—greater than 50%—and complete control over management. Stung by the Volvo affair, Louis Schweitzer and his Renault team adopted a much "softer" approach in their negotiations with Nissan. Instead of asking for exclusive discussions, Renault requested the establishment of an evaluative process that would involve more than a hundred individuals from each company. For many long months, the "Nissans" and the "Renaults" talked about their profession, their products, about platforms and engines, about technical or geographical synergies, and in the process got to know and appreciate one another. Money questions would be resolved later. The longer this mutual examination went on, the clearer it became to both sides that the "fit" between the two carmakers was nearly ideal. In the course of top-secret summit talks between Schweitzer and Hanawa, an evident chemistry developed between the former student at the École Nationale d'Administration (France's elite finishing school for managers) and the graduate of the University of Tokyo. In November 1998, Louis Schweitzer played his trump card. Carlos Ghosn, his second in command, who had been lured away from Michelin two years previously, went to Tokyo and made a blackboard presentation to Nissan's executive committee. The subject of the presentation was the "20 Billion Plan," which had enabled Renault to rebound spectacularly after a difficult year in 1996. Ghosn's demonstration had a significant impact on the later course of the negotiations. Hanawa now shared Schweitzer's conviction that Carlos Ghosn was the man the circumstances required. Nissan's executives were seduced, but not yet completely won over. They continued to hope for an accord with DaimlerChrysler and did not suspend their contacts with Ford.

Although negotiations had started late in the spring of 1998, the outcome was decided in the course of several weeks, between the middle of February and the end of March 1999. First came the sudden announcement that DaimlerChrysler was withdrawing from the field. Bogged down in a merger with Chrysler that was proving much more difficult than had been foreseen, Jürgen Schrempp was unable to persuade the American members of his board of directors to take advantage of this unique opportunity. He was committed to his formula of a "merger between equals" (though later he would bluntly admit in court that this principle had been nothing but a decoy) and refused to exert undue pressure.

Renault CEO Louis Schweitzer had an impressive dossier. After heavy losses in 1996, Renault had returned to profitability the following year. The company had no debt, a healthy hoard of cash, and a solid product line. The company had rejuvenated its managerial staff and was confident it had a staff who were ready, willing, and able to make a success of the proposed Japanese alliance. But Schweitzer had to convince his principal shareholder, the French government. An historical opportunity, a chance to assure the long-term future of the company, was at hand. It would require a change in dimension, in geographical horizon, in technological scale, in financial weight. The deal was not without risk, but it was a calculated risk, certainly less dangerous than sitting still in an industry where everything was in motion. Nevertheless, it would be an understatement to say that the past record of the government of France, in its role as shareholder in government-owned enterprises, was distinguished either for clarity of vision or for courage. In principle, government-owned companies in the business sector enjoyed the same freedom of management as their privately owned rivals. But in actual fact, the state-owned firms were expected to conduct themselves in a socially or politically "responsible" manner. Second, the handling of the state-owned businesses was often irresponsible. And finally, there was the question of political interference.

But Louis Schweitzer knew his way around this world. He was on familiar terms with many members of the current government, both ministers and advisers, starting with the prime minister, Lionel Jospin. Many of them had received the same education, and entered working life the same way: through the École Nationale d'Administration, which recruits and prepares its students for high public office. Schweitzer's dossier was scrutinized at the highest levels, properly, conscientiously, but with benevolence. And so the government, in its role as principal shareholder, authorized Renault's proposed strategic risk.

A SIGH OF RELIEF IN TOKYO

The administration and the government in Tokyo, too, wished to support the Renault-Nissan alliance. But this was no easy matter. Although Japanese corporations had for many decades been expanding internationally, this global outlook was coupled with an entrenched, long-standing hostility to foreign businesses penetrating the Japanese domestic market. In the mercantilist logic of Japan, exports, whether of products, factories, or capital, were a good thing; imports were an admission of weakness. Direct foreign investments, the powerful driving force behind the globalization movement that began in the 1980s, remained, so to speak, "persona non grata" in Japan. Friendly mergers were extremely rare, and hostile takeovers were impossible.

But the tectonic plates had shifted in Japan, as everywhere else. The colossal speculative bubble that had carried the stock exchange and the real estate market to fabulous heights began to collapse in the mid-1980s. Since then, unable to reform a growth model whose validity had largely expired, Japan had been paying the price for its former prosperity. By the beginning of the 1990s, the ex-champion of economic growth was bringing up the rear of industrialized nations. Japan didn't implode like an ordinary developing country—its accumulated reserves were too enormous for that—but its banking system suffered a mighty blow. Political instability, financial scandals, and deep-rooted cultural attitudes called into question a bureaucracy that had long been above suspicion, and the once watertight system was leaking like a sieve.

Unenthusiastically but systematically, Japan began a gradual transformation of its regulatory structure, its accounting norms, and its methods of business administration, adapting them to the principles established as international standards in Europe and the United States. The crisis shook the Japanese social contract to its foundations: lifetime employment; promotions based on seniority; the reciprocal, almost osmotic relationships between firms and oversight authorities; the time-honored, mutual cooperation woven into the *keiretsu* networks. Under the blows of necessity, the interlocking partnerships came apart. Conglomerates whose histories and rivalries even predated the Meiji reforms (which began in the late 1860s) merged their activities. And people began to entertain the idea that survival might entail rapprochement with a foreign business group.

There was, of course, a certain amount of hostile muttering, especially from the political and bureaucratic old guard, but the naming of Renault as Nissan's new principal stockholder was accepted with remarkable tolerance. After the initial surprise, the chief reaction in the Japanese press, as in the great majority of the international media, was skepticism. Few people were willing to bet that the undertaking would succeed.

"LE COST KILLER"

The Renault-Nissan Alliance now had a face. It belonged to a man born to Lebanese parents in Brazil and educated in France, whose professional itinerary covered Europe and the two American continents: Carlos Ghosn, known by the international press as "Le Cost

Killer." For eighteen years, Carlos Ghosn had worked for Michelin, the world's leading tire manufacturer; laboring in relative obscurity, he had climbed the corporate ladder at Michelin with record speed. In 1996, the year he accepted Louis Schweitzer's offer and joined Renault, he was the chief of Michelin's North American operations, responsible for some 40% of the company's worldwide sales.

At Renault's headquarters in Billancourt, Ghosn had been the principal architect of the 20 Billion Plan, the radical program of cost-cutting designed to revive Renault in 1996. Ghosn's plan required the closing of only one plant, the Renault factory in Vilvoorde, Belgium, although even that generated a great outcry. Despite heavy political pressure, Renault's management stood firm. The 20 Billion Plan was vigorously executed, and by 1997 Renault was profitable again. And so Carlos Ghosn earned his first nickname.

Renault had paid $5 billion to acquire 36.8% of Nissan's capital stock. The alliance agreement stipulated that three executives from Renault would form part of a ten-member board of directors. Carlos Ghosn would be the executive in charge of the Japanese company, with the title of Chief Operating Officer.

Nissan's employees were apprehensive. But Renault did not send an occupying army to Nissan's headquarters at Ginza. Rather, they sent at most a small commando squad; the first list of expatriate executives included only seventeen names. Louis Schweitzer's instructions to them were simple: Renault is neither very big nor very rich, so act quickly. Before leaving Paris, Carlos Ghosn had given his troops their orders. It was not a question of changing Japan, he said, but of helping Nissan get back on its feet.

SUCCESS STORY

And in fact, everything did go very fast. On October 18, 1999, the eve of the opening of the Tokyo Motor Show, Ghosn presented the Nissan Revival Plan, or NRP. The part of the plan that made the biggest headlines was the elimination of 21,000 jobs from

Nissan's worldwide operation (most of the layoffs were in Japan) and the closing of five factories. Traditional taboos fell by the wayside, as did illusions. "Nissan's in bad shape," Ghosn said that day. More unusual than this admission was the announcement that (1) Nissan would return to financial stability within a year of the implementation of the NRP; (2) within three years, its debt would be reduced by 50%; (3) also within three years, its operating margin would rise to 4.5% of sales. If these commitments were not fulfilled by the stipulated dates and at the stipulated levels, the members of the executive committee, including Ghosn himself, would hand in their resignations. The rest, as they say, is history—the history narrated in this book.

As it turned out, Carlos Ghosn and his team kept their commitments and retained their positions in Nissan's leadership; furthermore, under their direction, the revival of the Japanese carmaker became the most extraordinary success story of the automotive world in the new century. In a country where economic stagnation persists, in a domestic and international environment marked by a recession in the United States, the collapse of stock markets, and a general decline from the high stock values that dominated the 1990s, Nissan is thriving. The goals of the NRP were all reached before March 31, 2002. The succeeding plan, Nissan 180, was designed for growth: Within three years—that is, by the end of September of 2005—Nissan planned to increase its global sales by one million vehicles; in addition, by the spring of 2005 it was committed to achieving an operating margin of at least 8%, and reducing its net automotive debt to zero. In fiscal year 2003 (April 1, 2003–March 31, 2004), Nissan became the most profitable large automotive manufacturer in the world, with an operating profit margin of 11.1%. The company began hiring again. In a Japan suffering from deflation and falling salaries, Nissan was giving its employees raises. In the United States, Nissan invested more than a billion dollars to build a new factory; in China, Nissan spent another billion to purchase a 50%

interest in a company that seems destined to become a leader in the most promising automobile market on the planet. Nissan has rediscovered its ability and its will to make cars that people like, cars that turn heads in the street. The 350Z, a descendant of the legendary Datsun 240Z, is considered the standard-bearer of this rebirth. After years of uncertainty and neglect, a great enterprise has found its way again.

The credit for this goes to Renault, which took a risk that other companies, richer and more powerful, shied away from. The French manufacturer has already won its bet. The Renault-Nissan Alliance has allowed Renault to change dimension; once an essentially European manufacturer, Renault has transformed itself into one of the major players in the world automotive industry, with an indirect presence in the United States, expanding sales in Central America, South America, and throughout the Asia-Pacific region, and the imminent prospect of a large-scale operation in China. But the adventure is still young. Meanwhile, the bonds of the Renault-Nissan Alliance have been strengthened. In March 2002, Renault increased its share in Nissan's capital to 44.4%, and a few months later, thanks to a new divestment on the part of the French government, the Japanese manufacturer took a 15% share in Renault.

So far, however, the Alliance has delivered but a part of its potential. In the years ahead, the exchange of expertise and technical know-how, the integration of supply networks, the sharing of production capacities and global commercial infrastructures should yield further advances in efficiency, productivity, and profitability.

GLOBALIZATION WITH A HUMAN FACE

The foundation of this success lies in the relationships between the employees from Renault and those from Nissan, the rapport that exists among the men and women who carry on the daily work of the two companies. It's an intangible quality that only those with inside experience can describe. Their tale includes the incomprehension, impatience, trade-offs, tense moments, even confrontations, as well as the exhilaration and laughter, the highs and lows that have inevitably marked the rapprochement of two enterprises, two histories, two cultures that at first sight are completely different. The success has not been the result of luck or chance. It has come, first of all, because the leadership teams on both sides placed all their cards on the table from the start and dedicated themselves to the Alliance. In a speech given in Tokyo in spring 2001, Louis Schweitzer recalled the principles outlined in the Alliance Charter that he and Yoshikazu Hanawa signed in 1999: recognition of and respect for differences, mutual trust, open-mindedness, receptiveness. "These principles," he explained, "appear extraordinarily simple and natural, but if you look at a traditional management handbook, you'll see that some of them are missing. It's imperative for each side to preserve its own culture while at the same time making an effort to understand the other's culture and to adapt to it. We've chosen a way based on mutual respect and the acknowledgment of two enterprises and two identities."

The paradox is that the man who, more than anyone, has carried out this project is neither Japanese nor "classically" French. Born in Brazil into a family of Lebanese origin, educated in some of the best schools in France, Carlos Ghosn is the epitome of cultural diversity. Although many voices can be heard denouncing globalization these days, the shared adventure of Renault and Nissan offers a living demonstration of what globalization can accomplish when it is managed with consideration for people and respect for their individuality. Today, when company executives are regularly exposed to public contempt or thrust into the media limelight (usually, but not always, against their will), the story of *Shift* confirms the truism that man's real riches lie in the human heart. It shows that business enterprise is a crucible where people can join their talents, their efforts, and their passions in an attempt to better their common destiny.

SHIFT

CHAPTER 1

DEPARTURE

My grandfather, Bichara Ghosn, emigrated from Lebanon to Brazil when he was thirteen years old. He traveled alone. In those days, people left when they were still comparatively young. Going to school didn't seem so important.

At the time, the country was still part of the Ottoman Empire, which extended from Turkey to the Arabian Peninsula and the banks of the Nile. But it was an empire that was breathing its last. Distant and corrupt, Constantinople had trouble maintaining order in its far-flung provinces. There were several waves of emigration from Lebanon at the beginning of the twentieth century. The two primary reasons were conflicts based on religious differences—Druzes (a sect of Shi'a Islam) against Maronites, Sunnis against Shi'a—and endemic poverty. My grandfather came from Kesrouan, the part of Mount Lebanon that was 100% Maronite. The Maronites place a very high value on loyalty, especially loyalty to the Church, and respect for traditions. The Maronite mass has always been said in Syriac, for example. Although it's a language no one speaks anymore, it was the language Christ spoke. Maronite traditions and loyalty have been passed down from generation to generation. The Maronites who emigrated have maintained their loyalty to Lebanon and to their family members who stayed in the old country. They send money. They pay to construct a house in their ancestral village and visit it from time to time. The Lebanese Maronites are also loyal to France, which is the result of a long, nearly thousand-year-old history that goes back to the Crusades.

When you live in a world of constant menace, your close family circle is the one place where you're protected, where you can affirm your identity, which is always under threat from the Muslims, from invasions, and from the divisions between rival factions in Lebanon itself.

In the villages, the means of subsistence were limited, families were large, and land was scarce. The young had no prospects. Like so many others, my grandfather realized that he couldn't provide for himself if he stayed in Lebanon. One family member probably told him about a cousin or friend in Brazil, while another one spoke of someone he knew who'd gone to the United States and made his fortune.

"Making your fortune," of course, didn't mean becoming a millionaire; it meant finding a steady job, making enough income to begin and provide for a family, and assure the children a good education.

One fine day at the beginning of the twentieth century, my grandfather left his village, walked down the mountain, on his way to a ship in port at Beirut. After a crossing that took three months, he arrived in Rio de Janeiro, Brazil; he was nearly illiterate, he didn't have a cent, and he spoke only one language, Arabic.

Rio de Janeiro was the city where the people who'd made their money in the provinces went to take up residence and enjoy life. But the Brazilian El Dorado, at that time, was in the Amazon, in central and northwestern Brazil.

So Bichara shouldered his bag and set out for the new frontier, the territory of Guapore, near the border between Brazil and Bolivia. It later became the state of Rondonia, whose capital city, Porto Velho, lies on the Madeira River, one of the great tributaries of the Amazon River. It was there that he decided to set down his bag.

He went up and down the region, doing odd jobs. Little by little, he found his own way, started working for himself, and became an entrepreneur. At first, he bought and sold agricultural products; later, he went into the rubber trade. *Hevea brasiliensis*, the Brazilian rubber tree, was plentiful in those parts. Later still, he helped develop some of the Brazilian airlines that were establishing a countrywide network, acting as a local agent. He helped them to get to know the region and provided them with various services.

After many decades of hard work, in a country where he didn't know the language and started with nothing, he became the head of several companies. One of them traded in agricultural products, one of them was in the rubber business, and a third operated in air transport.

Although he is a very important person to me, I never knew my grandfather. I speak about him from hearsay, because he died relatively young at the age of fifty-three, long before I was born. He needed a gallbladder operation, and in those days, surgical resources in the Brazilian interior were primitive. He died on the operating table. But everyone who talked to me about him—my father, my uncles, and many other people who knew him—described him as a powerful personality. He was a genuine pioneer with a taste for taking risks. He had to make his way on his own when he was still very young, without money or knowledge or education. I admire him as someone who started with nothing, built himself a completely respectable life, educated his children properly, and left a decent inheritance, although quite small by today's standards.

But his inheritance bequeathed to his eight children, four boys and four girls, and his grandson was far more than his modest estate—they also inherited his example and his values.

He wasn't an ordinary man. He did some things that surprise me to this day. His contemporaries greatly respected him, and not only for his accomplishments. They admired him because he was a man of great integrity, a quality that was pretty rare in those days in the world of the pioneers. He was a man with principles and a family man; that's the way I think of him. His children were very attached to him. My father spoke of his father with a great deal of affection, as did my uncles and my aunts. He was someone who left a mark on their lives.

. . .

When my grandfather died, the family business was divided among his children. Many of them were already working for one or another of the companies. My father, Jorge, took over the businesses related to air travel.

Like most families in the Lebanese diaspora, our family maintained close ties to Lebanon. My grandfather's brothers and sisters and cousins stayed in Lebanon, as did his mother. Roughly every three years, our family returned to Lebanon.

Like many émigrés, my father went back to the old country to get married. When it's time for serious things in life, many émigrés try to reaffirm the old values and traditions—especially when it comes to marriage, where family and religious values play such a large part. On one of his trips back to Lebanon, my father had obtained an introduction to a very reputable family, and that's how he met my mother. They got married in Lebanon, and she returned to Brazil with him to work and start a family themselves.

My mother, Rose, who has been called Zetta all her life, also came from a large family. They lived in the Lebanese mountains in the northern part of the country. Her father had immigrated to Nigeria, where she was born. But the schools in Nigeria were less than ideal, and so at a very young age she was sent to school in Lebanon. It was a common story. Her father stayed in Africa to work. He sent money to his family and returned to Lebanon from time to time, every two years, to spend the summer with them, before going back to Nigeria. That still happens frequently today, not only in Lebanon but also in many other countries of emigration.

Zetta attended school with the Sisters of Besançon, one of the teaching orders that were the guardians of Catholic faith and French culture in Lebanon. For the Maronites of the Lebanon Mountains, France was something like a second home. My mother received a French education; she loves French culture and French music. For her, there's France, and then there's the rest of the world. Naturally, if you have a mother who's devoted to France, that's going to rub off on you. French culture runs deep in our family.

My mother and father took up residence in Porto Velho. It was there that my sister Claudine and I were born.

While the natural world around us was exotic, the climate was difficult. Mosquitoes, heat, humidity. Swimming in the river was out of the question. The water wasn't potable unless you boiled it before you drank it.

One day, the young girl who helped my mother around the house gave me some water that hadn't been boiled. I must have been around two. I got very sick, and I had a series of stomach disorders. The doctor told my mother, "If you want your child to have a normal life, you have to take him to a more temperate region, where daily conditions are easier and the water is healthier." My mother first took me to Rio, hoping I'd get better there. In fact, I did get a little better, but I was far from being completely cured. My father and mother decided that the only solution was for me to leave Brazil and live in Lebanon with my grandmother.

And so my family settled into a pattern typical of the Lebanese diaspora: My mother, sister, and I returned to Lebanon, while my father shuttled between Brazil and Lebanon. We lived the way a great many families do when the father goes to work in a difficult country. He earned enough money to place his family in another country, one where education is of a higher caliber and conditions are easier.

The Maronite community is one where feminine values are very strong, which obviously presents a contrast with the surrounding Arab world. The mother plays a very important role in the family and exercises a great deal of influence. There are many reasons why this is the case. It's often because the mother remains in Lebanon while the father works abroad. She becomes the authority figure. Father and mother relate to each other as equals. And considering many fathers' long absences, you can even say that the mother becomes the head of the family.

When we arrived in Beirut, I was six years old. I would remain in Lebanon until I was seventeen, finishing high school at a prestigious Jesuit institution, the Collège Notre-Dame.

Because my mother and father were Maronites, that is, Eastern Catholics, both of them were devout; my mother is still very observant. We lived in a traditional religious environment, but we were not fundamentalists. We're very much open to Islam and the other religions. In Lebanon, religion takes the place of cultural affiliation. There are the Druzes, the Sunnis, the Shi'a, the Maronites, the Greek Orthodox, the Armenian Catholics. Your religion is a major part of your identity. I've always had a religious consciousness. I've never felt it as a constraint but rather as a way of life.

In 1960, when we arrived in Beirut, it was a prosperous, vivacious, sunlit, charming city, beloved by tourists, as well as the financial center of the diaspora and of the other countries in the region. Lebanon was considered "the Switzerland of the Middle East." The problems caused by the strong Palestinian presence and the interference of Lebanon's neighbors, Israel and Syria, didn't begin until 1973. And the full-blown civil war—which divided Beirut in two and left barely a stone unturned in the city center—began two years after that, in 1975. I had graduated from high school four years earlier, in 1971.

My childhood was the beginning of a very stable period in my life. I went to the same school from the first grade to the last. The Jesuits played a large role in my formation. In their educational philosophy, discipline is very important, and competition equally so. There's a constant challenge, a grading system that encourages students to outdo one another. After all, the Jesuit order was the first multinational company in the world. And at the same time, the Jesuits are well known for promoting intellectual freedom.

In one class we had a professor of French literature, Father Lagrovole, a short, stout Frenchman, already aging but still very strict. He was not really a nice man—in fact, a bit haughty—but he had such a passion for French literature that we respected him very much. He would chant poetry, trying to make us hear the music. He was extraordinarily fascinating because he was so excited by what he was talking about.

He said to us, "If you find things complicated, it means you haven't understood them. Simplicity is the basis of everything." He seemed extraordinarily wise, as the priests often did. Their families were far away, they'd left their friends behind, and they lived to perform a single mission: to teach Lebanese children, or other children on the other side of the world, the French language. There was something about them that fascinated me—their devotion, their sincerity, their simplicity, their culture. I learned a lot from the Jesuits, and by the time I graduated I had a firm sense of discipline and organization, along with a taste for competition and for a job well done.

In retrospect, I was an exceptional student, but an undisciplined one. The latter trait was the despair of my mother. My mother believed a sense of duty was essential, along with levelheadedness, practicality, and discipline. As far as she was concerned, authorities were always right. When I was with the Jesuits, she was happy because I got very good grades. But at the same time, she was distraught at my rebelliousness. If I hadn't been a good student, I would have been in serious trouble.

While the Jesuits showed little pity to rowdy or mediocre students, they were much more tolerant of good students, even the rebellious ones.

So they put up with me. I did well in math and physics, but my real passions were history, geography, and languages.

One result of my family's history was that it exposed me to many languages. The first language I learned was Portuguese. By the time I arrived in Lebanon, I spoke Portuguese, a little French, and very little Arabic. At the Collège Notre-Dame, we studied French and Arabic. Learning languages quickly became one of my passions. The study of language is the best way of understanding the connections between peoples and cultures. Today, English is my primary means of communication, although the language most familiar to me is still French.

I graduated from high school at the age of seventeen, having passed both my French *baccalauréat*, a necessity for gaining entrance into the French universities, and its Lebanese equivalent. When it was time to think about a college education, I was naturally drawn to France. While the United States was a possibility, I wasn't familiar with the school system, and American universities were very expensive.

I had no idea what it was I wanted to do with my life—I had no role models around me that I could follow. But we did have one cousin who had gone on to study business at the Hautes Études Commerciales and worked in a bank in Paris. During my last year in high school, I sent him my résumé and transcripts and asked him to enroll me in a preparatory school so I could enter the HEC, too.

And so I moved to Paris.

CHAPTER 2

PARIS

In spite of my fluency in French, my familiarity with French culture, and my French education, my arrival in Paris was something of a shock to me. It seemed enormous. I'd just come from Beirut, a sunny, pleasant city on the sea, and I found myself in a city that's still very beautiful, but also a little dark, a little more heavy. People are tougher in Paris, and their relations with one another are a bit impersonal.

I was admitted to the Lycée Saint-Louis on Boulevard Saint-Michel, one of the great French preparatory schools. For an alumnus of the Jesuits, the natural choice for me would have been the Collège Sainte-Geneviève, called familiarly "Ginette." But the fathers in Beirut had not been able to get over my past unruliness, and they advised against my admission. At first, I was placed in a boarding school, the Collège Stanislas on Rue Notre-Dame-des-Champs, on the edge of the Montparnasse quarter, where the students had their own rooms.

But the principal of the Lycée Saint-Louis was impressed by my grades in mathematics and thought I was wasting my ability preparing for the HEC, the advanced business school. He recommended that I enter the Lycée Saint-Louis as a *taupin* (a special mathematics student) and prepare for admission to the École Polytechnique, the top engineering university in Paris, where the best math students went.

In order to pass the highly competitive entrance examinations for the École Polytechnique, Lycée students have to completely dedicate themselves to their studies. The curriculum, called the *taupe*, is so demanding and intensive that students rarely stick their heads outside. The term focuses on the sciences and involves two years of preparation. The course of study is also called "higher mathematics" (*Maths Sup*), followed by "special mathematics" (*Maths Spé*). Mathematical excellence is the primary criterion for success.

My first trimester was a disaster. I'd never received a grade that was lower than the average, and here I was getting a four out of ten in mathematics. I failed for the first time in my life. I was in complete despair. I had to make some adjustments, because the way they taught mathematics in the *taupe* at that time was rather different from what I was used to. In Lebanon, we'd studied a lot of geometry, not much algebra, and very little modern algebra. In France, they taught algebra and topology.

Instead of giving up the *taupe*, I told myself I had to make a greater effort. I was determined to go on, no matter what it took; I wanted to show that I could do better than my grades indicated. By the end of *Maths Sup*, I was near the top of my class. This meant that I could continue preparing for Polytechnique.

The ten best students in each class were granted admission to section M, where they prepared for the entrance exam to the École Polytechnique. The next ten could go on to section M, but they would be prepared for other scientific schools, rather than the École Normale Supérieure (the elite training school for teachers) or the École Polytechnique. If you were one of the students bringing up the rear, you could hope to find your way into section P, the physics section.

I finished the last trimester at the head of the class. From that point on, the course I had to follow was quite clear: *Maths Sup* to *Maths Spé*, then the École Polytechnique, and finally the École des Mines.

After graduation from Polytechnique, an engineering university, ideally one would complete his or her education in a graduate school of applied science. The two that attracted the best students in each graduating class were the École des Mines (for mining studies) and the École des Ponts et Chaussées (for civil engineering).

I never entertained going to the École Normale Supérieure, because that track led to a teaching career. I would certainly have been interested in teaching history and geography, but not mathematics. For my classmates, my fellow *taupins*, Polytechnique was Mecca, and I caught their enthusiasm. Polytechnique gave you the possibility of steering your career in the direction you wanted. When you got out, you could go to graduate school in education or you could continue in science. I told myself that it would be a good challenge, and at the same time I'd remain free to choose my career. At Polytechnique, you're furthering your education, but you still have time to think about what you want to do later. By contrast, the specialized schools set you on predetermined tracks very soon—too soon, in my opinion.

Historically (though it's much less true today), this meritocracy in the French style functioned as a powerful engine of cultural assimilation. The Grandes Écoles attracted the best foreign students, especially those who came from countries that were former French colonies; but whatever his family or national origins, the student who overcame the various academic obstacles saw the gates to professional success and ascension in the social hierarchy open before him.

In Polytechnique, I had some friends whose fathers were gym teachers or elementary school teachers, a few—not many—who were the children of working-class people, and about an equal number whose fathers held high positions in industry. But the school made us all equal. There was very little preening or showing off. In France, people don't boast about their origins too much. They try to fit in and be like the others in the university system.

In Lebanon, I was peculiar because I was born in Brazil and spoke Portuguese. I wasn't a "total" Lebanese; I was a native of another country, and I had no plans to live and work in Lebanon. Then I went to France, and I was peculiar there, too. At the Lycée Saint-Louis, a Brazilian birth certificate and a diploma from a Lebanese high school made me rather distractingly different from the average *taupin*, who came to school from his home in the fifth *arrondissement*. I've always been someone who was different. I've never lived in a place where I could tell myself I was an integral part of the group like everyone else.

On the other hand, when you're a child, you don't like being different. You want to be like the others. I went through some difficult moments. But what happens is that you learn to surmount these difficulties in your childhood, and so you're armed for the future. Once you're an adult, being different isn't a problem anymore. Your defenses are already up. In France, people feel very attracted to whatever's different. There's a lot of curiosity. But even though French culture is very open, at the same time it's also very structured. The French are quite curious about the rest of the world, but they're also quite proud of being French, of having a way of life that's unique to France. They don't want foreigners to become like them, but they greatly prefer a foreigner who tries to fit in smoothly. It's both difficult and easy. It allows you to be yourself, even as you're sharing in the French way of life. At the École Polytechnique, I never felt ostracized in any way. But I knew I was different, and the others knew it, too.

Outside the classrooms, student life in Paris in my time revolved around several familiar places in the Latin Quarter: the libraries, especially Sainte-Geneviève, which faces the Panthéon; the various university restaurants, known as *les restau U*; and the movie houses. I was a great fan of the movies, and Paris was an extraordinary city for a cinemaphile. My tastes were quite broad. Attending the movies was an important focus of student life, along with the many libraries in that part of the city. And, of course, eating at the *restau U*, which was an institution and a monument. A student meal ticket was worth two and a half francs, I believe. You had to eat as much as possible so you could make it through the long days of classes and studying. Some of *les restau U* were three-star places—relatively speaking, of course—and in some of the others you had to force yourself to eat what they brought you. But we were hardly rich. We lived on math courses, first at Polytechnique and later at École des Mines. Food wasn't our biggest concern, but you had to eat enough to sustain yourself.

My class at Polytechnique was the second-to-last on Mount Sainte-Geneviève before the school moved out to Palaiseau. It was a wonderful place. I lived in Paris for seven years, from 1971 to 1978, and I spent the whole time in a relatively small area that goes from Rue Notre-Dame-des-Champs, where Stanislas is, to Mount Sainte-Geneviève and the École des Mines on Boulevard Saint-Michel. I know that part of town by heart: the bistros, the restaurants, the cinemas. For seven years, I roamed around inside that little perimeter.

The students at X—the nickname for École Polytechnique—received a stipend. And there was no shortage of ways to supplement one's income. I gave courses in mathematics. In fact, student life in a prestigious university in France is quite pleasant. I particularly remember a trip I took with my classmates to the United States. We went to attend a seminar on American culture; before we got to the place where the seminar was being held—the University of Colorado, in Boulder—we traveled all over the country. There were about forty of us from Polytechnique, and we arrived on the campus just at the time when the Martha Graham Dance Company was in training there. Young women were dancing outside on the grass. We were transfixed.

Back at X, as part of my interest in learning languages, I organized a *table américaine*. We invited American students who were living in Paris. We ate dinner together at X twice a month to practice our English. Afterward, we'd end the evening in the bars and nightclubs of the Latin Quarter.

The civil war that broke out in Lebanon in 1975 provoked a reunion of our family in Paris. The war broke out just as I was finishing up at Polytechnique and about to enter École des Mines. My older sister, Claudine, was already in Paris doing graduate work in ethnology. The rest of the family came to France when the war broke out. The war affected me, naturally, but it wasn't like living in Lebanon. Fortunately, I was in France and I had a Brazilian passport; I wasn't a prisoner somewhere in Lebanon. The civil war was the signal for yet another wave of emigration. A great many Lebanese left the country and settled in Paris or elsewhere in Europe, while others went to the United States or to other Arab countries.

My grades at Polytechnique were sufficiently high for me to be admitted to the École des Mines, the most prestigious of the so-called *écoles d'application*, the "applied science schools." The engineers who graduated from the École des Mines tended to assume executive positions in the administrations of major companies.

There are two tracks: the students in one become civil servants, and the students in the other are free to do what they wish after they graduate. I was never on the civil servant track. I was considering doing further study in economics and getting a postgraduate certificate.

If you're a student at Polytechnique, your life revolves primarily around mathematics. People work hard so that they can get a position in a big government job. Ideally, it serves as a springboard to a good state-supported organization. But I had absolutely nothing to do with that. It never even crossed my mind to consider becoming a civil servant.

The French educational system was based on competition, selection, and your ability to showcase your intelligence. Teamwork? Forget it! Ideally, you wanted to show yourself as one of the brilliant guys who know how to come up with the easiest solutions to the most complicated math problems. The more abstract something was, the more appreciation your work received. There was little connection between the real business world and what was taught in the universities.

My education gave me a great deal, including the ability to move quickly from one issue to another and grasp the essential points, a fondness for precision, an aversion to approximation, and the resources to take up intellectual challenges. I learned the value of hard work, the necessity of discipline and organizational skills.

When I began my professional career, what I encountered was nothing like what I'd been taught. The Grandes Écoles may have prepared us to become high-ranking civil servants, but they didn't teach us anything about becoming good entrepreneurs. When I started at Michelin, everyone knew I'd gone to Polytechnique and the École des Mines. That made a favorable impression at first, but I had to build from the bottom up; I had to learn everything from scratch.

CHAPTER 3

MICHELIN

When I received a call from an executive at Michelin, I hadn't given much thought to my future. But the call from Michelin shook me. I hadn't intended to join a big company. I was in my last year at the École des Mines, planning to work toward a postgraduate certificate in economic science. I was twenty-four, making a decent living giving special mathematics classes to Lycée students. I was content, and I intended to think about my professional life at some later date. I was a bachelor, and the life of a student in Paris is extraordinary in every way.

Michelin wanted a Brazilian engineer with a French education to work in Rio de Janeiro. Brazil had always been on my mind when I was in Lebanon and France. I'd always told myself that I would make my career in Brazil. It was what I'd prepared for. I figured my best opportunities would be in Brazil. I'd spent the first five years of my life there, and the land and its language were always in my thoughts. I've always considered Brazil the country of the future.

Brazil is a beautiful, fascinating, generous country, an extraordinary melting pot. I love it. Even today, after all this time, I still think of Rio as the one city in the world where I feel most comfortable. Although my father died in June 2002, my mother still lives in Rio, and so do two of my sisters.

There was never a question of my going back to Lebanon. Torn apart by civil war, the country was on the verge of self-destruction. And I never intended to settle in France. In France, there was nothing distinctive about me. In France, your value is determined by your diplomas. But in Brazil, a country where foreign investment was about to expand rapidly, I knew I would enjoy many professional advantages, including my French education and my knowledge of French culture. Many French companies were beginning to set up shop in Brazil. It seemed only natural that I should seize an opportunity to return to Brazil as an executive with a French firm.

Admittedly, I was rationalizing something that was fundamentally emotional. What I really wanted was to reconnect with Brazil, with my childhood. So when Michelin called me and said the words "Brazilian project," everything clicked into place. It seemed like fate. It was the only possibility that could have torn me away from my studies and my student life. Their proposal offered me all sorts of advantages: an entry into industry, a French corporation with a global vision, and a return to Brazil, where my family was.

Two weeks later, I traveled to Clermont-Ferrand, where I met several of Michelin's top executives. Two or three weeks later, they presented me with a very attractive contract.

The people at Michelin told me, "To begin with, we must train you in France. When your training's over, you'll leave for Brazil. Your starting position will depend, in part, on the progress you make in France." Their offer was extremely attractive. Moreover, the project was based in Rio, not São Paulo. I decided it was exactly right for me, and it made sense out of everything I'd done up to that point.

The company had been born in Clermont-Ferrand, the capital of the Auvergne, in the heart of the Massif Central, at the end of the nineteenth century. All the oldest factories in town were located in the city center; Michelin was by far the biggest employer in the region. When the sons of Michelin workers grew up, they got jobs at Michelin. The company accompanied its employees, as the saying went, "from the maternity ward to the cemetery." It housed generations of its workers in company flats, educated them in its schools, and trained them in its training centers. One became a Michelin employee for life. The proprietary family, in characteristic Auvergnat fashion, was known for its austere lifestyle and its absolute discretion.

Michelin had a good reputation. The only downside was leaving Paris and moving to Clermont-Ferrand, which was not exactly a fun place. I consoled myself with the thought that I wouldn't be there long. A year of training, and I'd be off to Brazil. As it turned out, I stayed in Europe until 1985. Seven years!

The company uses a fairly unusual but very effective system for integrating young university graduates into their new jobs. It's called PS—personnel service—training. All the new hires go through this training, which lasts three months. Everyone shares the same living quarters and offices. Instructors take the new recruits under their wing, and for three months they attend lectures given by the company's chief executives. The lectures cover various subjects: production, commerce, finance, sales, international markets, and so on. This process allows the recruits to get to know the company and the people in charge of it, the people at the top.

Their method was very effective in smoothing the transition from student life to life in the business world. Moreover, the training process instilled in newcomers an appreciation for the distinctive character of the Michelin enterprise.

I started in September 1978. Generally, PS training classes that form in September are filled with young people, because that's when the new university graduates start work. My class was unusually large—about a hundred, if I remember correctly. These new Michelin employees included engineers, salespeople, people with degrees in marketing or finance, personnel experts, and so on. It made for a very good mix. When you're all starting work for the same company, you feel a natural solidarity; we shared our experiences—problems, difficulties, and jokes. What happens is that bonds are formed between us, and then they spread throughout the company and help create a kind of network for each of us. The atmosphere was very relaxed, very friendly. Most of us were graduates of one of the universities in Paris; this was our first contact with industry—with a tire manufacturer, at that—and it was a shock. But the shock was quite a lot easier to bear when you shared it with a large group of people very much like you, with a background and qualifications much the same as yours.

I established friendships that lasted throughout my career at Michelin and have continued to this day.

New employees in training attended a series of lectures; at the same time, they were given problems to solve. These weren't made-up academic problems but real operational questions that arose in the company.

You dealt with one, two, or three problems, according to how fast you could handle them. This method gave you an opportunity to find appropriate solutions even as you were discovering the company for yourself. At the same time, it gave the company a chance to find out about you; when you're in PS training and you show up in a manufacturing shop to analyze a problem and deal with it, you are under scrutiny from every angle.

In one shop there was an autoclave, a kind of giant cooking-pot that wasn't being sufficiently utilized. They asked me, "Should we shut it down, or should we spend money and modernize it?" I went around to the shop to see what the people were up to with their autoclave. I also went to the nearby shops to see whether or not the thing might be useful to them as well. Then I made my report, which concluded with a recommendation to keep the autoclave and to make use of it in a more rational, systematic way. This experience enabled me to become acquainted with several shops inside Michelin's big factory in Clermont-Ferrand.

My second case brought me into contact with the most precious resource in the tire industry: latex, extracted from trees of the genus *Hevea* all over the world and used in the manufacture of rubber. The question I had to solve had to do with employee safety. Latex arrived at the factory in tanks. A worker was assigned to climb up on the tank and get a sample of the latex, which would be checked to make sure it met the factory's specifications. I was asked to evaluate what could be done to improve working conditions and make that employee's job safer. The problems we were presented with didn't have much to do with grand strategies. We were confronted with very concrete, very detailed questions that required us to come into contact with many people in our search for a practical solution.

The head of PS training when I went through it was René Zingraff, who later became the third-ranking manager in the company. At the time, he was also my own personal mentor. As you progressed in your training, reports started coming in from everywhere: "We saw young Ghosn. He's not bad," or "He's irritating," or "He's a nice guy," or "He gives himself airs," and so on. And all these reports found their way to your mentor in PS training.

By the end of three months, Michelin had no doubt formed certain ideas about me, and the reverse was true as well. I liked what I saw at Clermont-Ferrand. Michelin, I thought, is better than its reputation suggests. The external image of the company was certainly out of line with the reality. Michelin had an incredibly modern outlook. Later, that would become a permanent feature of the company. The fact that I was given great responsibilities when I was still very young; the fact that I was able to carry out my responsibilities in France like everyone else, even though I wasn't French; the fact that we were able to establish direct working relationships with the chief executives of the company, and that we were encouraged to discuss problems openly, no matter who might be displeased—all this showed Michelin's modern, even avant-garde attitude, which was nowhere reflected in its reputation. There was a discrepancy between Michelin's public image and the reality that I experienced there.

Michelin revolutionized the tire industry shortly after the end of World War II by producing the first radial tires. Since this breakthrough, the French firm has always fought hard to be a technological leader. Today, it is one of the top three tire corporations in the world.

The head of Michelin, François Michelin, the third generation of the founding family, didn't learn to do what he did in textbooks on management. His openness to giving young executives great responsibility, his indifference to their origins, and the attention he paid to facts rather than theories were all manifestations of François Michelin's personality.

Very tall, slightly stooped, modestly dressed, and extremely courteous, François Michelin headed the company for more than forty years, turning the company from what was basically a domestic firm into a multinational corporation. He has a strong tendency to focus on individuals. He's not at all oriented toward large groups. And he also pays a lot of attention to the facts, to reality. These traits are discernible inside the company. I saw a firm that's fairly simple in the way it functions, austere in its business practices, and focused on its individual employees, on its products, and on quality control. Problems are confronted as they arise, and Michelin makes a real effort to approach each one without resorting to foregone conclusions and without respect for taboos.

When PS training ended, the new employees passed into another training phase relating to their specialty. I was chiefly interested in the factory shops. I wanted to exchange my Polytechnique uniform for blue overalls.

From the onset, I had asked to be assigned to manufacturing. When they offered me a contract, it stipulated that I would go into research. I told them that I didn't join Michelin to become a tire specialist. I wanted to make my contribution to the framework of this industry, and I thought the best place to do that was in production. That's where everything happens. You have to know the product, the people who make it, and the management. In the end, they agreed to my request.

The PS training lasts three months, long enough to show whether your personal style matches the company's style, whether or not you're a good fit in the shop, whether you get along with the workers, the foremen, the technicians.

The first three months of my training was as a factory worker. I didn't make tires. I worked in a prep shop, where we prepared the rubber that was going to be used to make them. I cut up rubber, put it in molds, rolled it up, and transported it, among other things. The trainees accepted this labor assignment gracefully, more or less. As far as I was concerned, it was part of the rules of the game, and I really loved that part of the training. First of all, I knew it was a unique occurrence—I wasn't going to go back sometime down the road and work in that shop. That knowledge let me observe how the workers did their jobs. I saw what kind of relations they had with the foremen and how technology was applied to factory operations. I started to see how to improve operational quality. It was a very interesting period. Michelin used a three-eight system—a daily rotation of three eight-hour work shifts. I worked them all. When I was on the morning shift, I had to get up at four to be at the factory at five. I also worked the afternoon shift, which started at one, and the night shift.

There was a real camaraderie on the shop floor. If a trainee was friendly with the workers, if he ate with them and played cards with them during the breaks, there was no problem. What the workers couldn't stand was someone who held himself aloof. That was not the case with me.

I had a monitor who worked with me. At the end of each shift, he gave me some additional instruction to help me study operation systems. Since he wanted to get ahead in the company himself, he'd applied to take some math tests, and I helped him prepare for them. So we spent an extra hour together, and we divided it in half: thirty minutes for me, and thirty minutes to discuss his math problems. It was very pleasant, and we established a solid bond.

Soon, I was promoted to shift team leader at the factory in Puy-en-Velay, where Michelin makes its biggest tires, some of them several meters high, which are an essential feature of heavy equipment. These are the tires used on the biggest machines on a work site, the scrapers and dumpers and earthmovers. I spent a lot of time in the shop. Team leaders evaluated productivity and work organization. I tried to improve product flow and eliminate some practices that didn't make sense in the overall organizational plan. In those kinds of situations, you realize the importance of teaching skills, education, and communication between the manager and the workers in the shop. Even the best organizational ideas are worth nothing if they aren't communicated and supported clearly, with a thoroughly concrete explanation of why and how. I had received zero preparation for this sort of thing, but the questions that arose were really just matters of simple common sense. You didn't need a degree from Polytechnique to figure it out.

After six months at Puy-en-Velay, I was sent to Germany for training as a quality-control technician in the Michelin factory in Karlsruhe. After that, I returned to France, where I was trained in industrial organization at the factory in Tours. Then came my first "real" job: head of the production team at the Cholet factory, where I spent the entire year in 1980.

The beginning of the 1980s was a period of strong growth at Michelin. High-level positions were coming open at a pretty rapid rate. The company was getting ready to expand in Brazil. An Asian operation was under way. The United States market was being developed. Executives only slightly senior to me were getting overseas assignments, and the newcomers had to be trained quickly. If a young person showed signs of enthusiasm and interest, he didn't have to wait long before he found himself in a position of responsibility.

Michelin's management raided the company's factories for

administrators to head its international operations. But the firm was having trouble finding the right general manager for its new plant in Puy, where I had previously trained as a shift team leader.

Roger Porte, who was the head of all the Michelin factories in France, had gone through a list of candidates. Later, he told me that mine was the last name on the list. He rejected all the others, but someone told him, "You should consider Carlos Ghosn. He's young, he hasn't been with the company long, but he seems pretty good." Porte called me in and said, "All right, I'm making you a factory boss." So, early in 1981, at the age of twenty-seven, I became general manager of the Michelin factory in Puy-en-Velay.

I was a very young manager in a young factory. It was, in fact, a fine factory, the newest plant in Europe in the Michelin family. My team was fairly young because the factory in Puy had been in operation for only a few years. Most of the workers were about my age. We had six hundred employees manufacturing giant tires for specialized heavy equipment. The employees were surprised to see me come back as general manager of the factory only a year and a half after serving as a shift-team leader, but it was, I think, a pleasant surprise. They knew they could discuss things with me. The workers in the shop were well disposed toward me, and I benefited from that. As for the management team, well, I was its youngest member, so that created a bit of disorder. The head of personnel was fifty-four. The head of production had been my boss when I was shift team leader. In the beginning, this made for some discomfort, but everybody gets over that sort of thing when they see that you're there to make things work.

The learning experience I had in Puy would decisively affect my later career. When you take charge of a factory, especially if you're young, you have to establish bonds. You have to spend time with the entire management team in order to introduce yourself, make acquaintances, identify the main problems they're working on, and understand the solutions they've come up with. So the first thing to do is to create a team.

The general manager of a factory isn't like the head of a line of products. The manager has much less room to maneuver. We had limited goals in quality control, in material losses, in productivity. The top brass in Clermont-Ferrand pretty much controlled everything. The important rules were decreed by the main office, and one had to try to obtain the best results possible while operating under these constraints.

The factory was running well, but it was subject to great fluctuations in productivity. The market for these tires is very cyclical. Either you find yourself running out of supplies or, conversely, you're technically out of work because you've made much more than the market demands. The way to cushion the impact of these wild variations was to improve organization and efficiency, but without doing damage to the goodwill that prevailed in the factory.

We did a pretty good job of solving our problems. It was a nonunionized factory. Its first boss, Camille Héaulmé, nicknamed "Rackham the Red," had created an atmosphere where there was no need for intermediaries, and I was able to preserve that spirit.

Two years later, early in 1983, while still general manager of the Michelin factory in Puy, I was summoned to the main office in Clermont-Ferrand. During my previous three and a half years with the firm, I had encountered François Michelin at company gatherings, but this was our first private meeting.

François Michelin was a legend in the company. The workers from Clermont-Ferrand called him "Monsieur François," but for everyone else he was simply "the Boss." Everyone knew whom you were talking about. There were three managing partners, but only one Boss.

François Michelin's office on the Place des Carmes in Clermont-Ferrand was a reflection of its owner: very simple, spare, even austere, a bit old-fashioned, and in impeccable order.

François Michelin is, above all, an inquisitive man, a man who's curious about other people. He's totally indifferent to what diplomas you've picked up or where you come from, but he's interested in who you are. He knew how to put me instantly at ease by talking about simple things—my family, my work, the company. He was very well informed, but he wasn't a man who read dossiers. He'd learned what he knew about me in discussions with his most trusted advisors. He wasn't the sort of man who would request a thirty-page biography—that wasn't his style at all. Furthermore, whatever he had been told about someone was less important than the impression he formed for himself.

Our interview lasted about an hour, perhaps an hour and a half.

We chatted a bit about a variety of subjects. He asked me to tell him what I thought about the company. And soon he brought the conversation around to the Kléber problem, which was obviously causing him a great deal of concern. Originally, Kléber-Colombes had been one of Michelin's competitors in the days before the consolidation of the tire industry. Michelin had taken financial control of Kléber while allowing it to lead a relatively independent existence. But Kléber was doing poorly, and the relationship was becoming an embarrassment for the Michelin group. He frankly described the fix the company was in, and then he said, "But one thing we can't do is to abandon Kléber. Could you study the situation and submit some suggestions?"

Upon leaving, I knew I was going to have to work hard, and fast.

François Michelin always had a strategic approach to problems. You had to work within a certain number of broad parameters, boundaries set according to his personal convictions, but apart from that he left you totally free to come up with tactical proposals.

So, in June 1983, I left the factory in Puy and went to work in Michelin's headquarters in Clermont-Ferrand, where I was transferred to analyze the Kléber situation with Behrouz Chahid-Nourai, the chief financial officer of the corporation.

Kléber manufactured automobile tires, as well as tires for vans and farm equipment. I prepared a complete analysis of the company and submitted my report in October. I had found that Kléber's position in the market for farm equipment tires was much stronger than Michelin's. This was an important asset. Kléber and its factories knew a lot about manufacturing tires for farm machinery, so it seemed like a good idea for them to make Michelin's farm tires, too.

On the basis of this first strategic analysis, I came up with an idea that would serve me well in various future circumstances: the principle known as "cross-manufacturing," utilizing the same production line for the manufacture of products sold under two or more different brands.

I recommended that Kléber's automobile tire business be folded into Michelin to be positioned as the Michelin group's budget brand.

Almost all my suggestions were implemented. But I wasn't able to see them through to the end, because in November 1983 Michelin offered me the directorship of a research-and-development group. They'd been nursing this idea since I first joined the company. I accepted the offer, and I went to the research center in Ladoux as head of the heavy-duty tire division, the group that produced tires for heavy equipment and farm machinery and industrial vehicles.

At Michelin, research was taken very seriously. Ever since its radial tire breakthrough, Michelin had been a technology leader in the industry. The work of the research group was monitored with a watchful eye by the Boss himself—François Michelin's principal areas of interest were products and research. The company allocated substantial budgets for research; it was always a top priority. The specifications were not open to discussion. Quality control, relations with the manufacturers—these were the Boss's personal domain, and everyone knew it.

The quality of a tire—its endurance, its adhesion to the road, its resistance to shocks—depends partly on its architecture but especially on the composition, cooking, and trimming of the rubber. If this sounds like a culinary recipe, it does require as much art as science.

The proper mix of natural rubber, synthetic rubber, and carbon black; the correct quantities and proportions of the ingredients; the appropriate finishing touches—all this requires experimentation, rather as a cooking recipe does. The formulas are closely held trade secrets. They form part of the company's vast body of expertise. Not even the factory bosses got access to the chemical formulas, which came directly from the laboratories in Clermont-Ferrand and were jealously guarded.

But I didn't stay in the laboratory long. Early in 1985, I received yet another assignment.

The news from Michelin's Brazil operation had started turning bad in November 1984. Behrouz Chahid-Nourai, the company's head of finance, told me, "Things are going badly in Brazil. We've invested heavily, but we're not making any profits. I'll be surprised if you stay in your present position very long. We have to fix the Brazil situation or we're going to be in serious trouble."

Behrouz Chahid-Nourai played an important role in my professional growth. He implanted in me an original approach to modern finance, which at the time was starting to occupy an increasingly important place in multinational corporations. Far from the image of the "bean counter" popularly attached to a firm's chief accountant, the chief financial officer must be a creative person, charged with the ongoing task of optimizing the company's resources and cash, and coordinating its appeals to the capital markets and banks.

Behrouz came from outside the company and brought with him a breath of fresh air—new ideas, new patterns, new ambitions. He was the one who taught me the importance of finance in an enterprise. Blessed with a quick, agile intellect, he was very open-minded. His good nature was always apparent, even as he introduced financial rigor and innovation into Michelin.

In January 1985, Michelin's board announced a shakeup in the management of its Brazilian operations. Seven years after joining the company, I was about to return to my native land.

I needed to exercise patience for a few more months, during which I continued to carry out my responsibilities in research and development while attending company meetings on the subject of Brazil. At last, in July 1985, I left for Brazil, where the situation was critical.

CHAPTER 4

RIO DE JANEIRO

I didn't return to Rio alone. My new wife, Rita, was by my side. I had first met Rita in September 1984 in Lyon, where she was studying pharmacy.

Rita was from Lebanon. My marriage renewed my ties with Lebanon. Her parents, her brothers and sisters, and her cousins all live in Lebanon. She goes back more often than I do, although from time to time she takes me along with her. We were married in Clermont-Ferrand in June, and early in July we left for Rio. She was twenty, I was thirty-one. For her, going to live in Brazil was an adventure—marriage, a new life. In fact, she's never had any difficulty adapting in any of the countries we've lived in.

At the time of our arrival, my father was living in retirement in Rio de Janeiro, surrounded by most of our family. Two of my three sisters had already returned to Brazil.

On the professional level, however, I wasn't expecting a party. I had been sent to Brazil because Michelin was in crisis.

Perennially on the verge of greatness and prosperity, Brazil, the giant of South America, a country with practically unlimited natural resources, has always been as disappointing as it is fascinating. Its economic history follows the cycles of its raw materials—wood, rubber, coffee, petroleum—which enrich the country and permit the growth of vast fortunes, only to plunge it into crisis when the wind changes.

Brazilians are very nationalistic. They feel a deep attachment to their homeland; at the same time, they're very self-critical. They have a great deal of difficulty assimilating in other countries. They're not happy anywhere else. Brazil's rich human resources, on the other hand, are a result of its own considerable powers of assimilation. They have enabled the country to absorb successive waves of immigrants successfully, without major upheavals and without the discrimination typically found elsewhere. Poles, Italians, Germans, "Turcos," descendants of African slaves. It's a very joyful, very easygoing culture, but in the past these qualities have always prevented it from surpassing itself, and they continue to make progress difficult today. That's why Brazil is both fascinating and irritating.

It's very exciting to be in a country that's moving into the future, even if that movement has already been under way for a long time. But even when you're young, the future doesn't last. The country has enormous potential: its great size, its natural resources, its environmental abundance. At the same time, however, it's extremely hard to achieve progress there. Still, although Brazil induces a certain level of weariness, its attractions are hard to resist.

On the economic front, hyperinflation, which distorts companies' profit-and-loss statements, was ravaging the country. I saw annual inflation rates higher than 1,000%, with real interest rates above 35%. The actual cost of money came to more than 350% annually.

After an initial infusion of capital, Michelin had hoped that its Brazilian division would finance its own investments. That didn't turn out to be true. Losses were transformed into debts, and when both inflation and interest rates are very high, the financial hole you're in gets deeper very fast.

We had to adjust salaries twice a month. We were burdened with price controls. If you missed the price adjustments by one or two days, the company's profit margin disappeared. You couldn't afford to make a mistake.

We had a factory in Campo Grande that produced heavy

equipment tires, another one in Resende that made the metal cables used in the manufacture of radial tires, and two rubber plantations, one in the Mato Grosso and one in the state of Bahia.

The plantations and factories were two completely different enterprises, and they were completely separate on an operational level. Planting trees, caring for them, collecting the latex and preparing it—none of this has anything to do with the manufacture of tires. But natural rubber was a raw material of such importance to Michelin that it would have been unthinkable for the company not to have control over its rubber supply.

Michelin's situation had deteriorated a great deal not only because of the country's economic environment, but also because management had so little comprehension of the situation. This is no small thing. You have to take that economic environment into account. You also have to consider what level of comprehension the management of the company brings to that economic circumstance, and what steps it must take to protect itself from it. And that part is an internal affair. If company executives have never lived in hyperinflationary conditions, accompanied by very finicky state regulations—price controls, financial controls, controls on imports, subsidies for exports—management runs the risk of making lots of stupid mistakes without even realizing it.

Moreover, we were under pressure from the head office; the rising losses in Michelin's Brazilian operation caused a certain panic in Clermont-Ferrand.

The solution was essentially a managerial one. There were some practices that had to be modified. To begin with, people from the head office who understood nothing about our Brazilian operation had to stop interfering. We said to them, "We accept all responsibility. Let us do our job, and then you can judge the results." Some Michelin executives in Clermont-Ferrand were panicking and giving terrible advice. Since the people on the ground in Brazil were a pretty disciplined lot, they followed headquarters' advice, even when they knew it was wrong.

The second priority was to put a genuine team in the field.

Michelin's Brazilian operation was composed of a great many separate divisions. We had manufacturers, retailers, financial specialists, and planters, and each of them worked in his own sphere. They all knew that I was a very different sort of manager from my predecessor, and they were quite aware that I was stepping into a crisis situation with the potential for dramatic consequences. So they went along with our game plan. We started having executive meetings to bring the top directors of each division together.

We realized that Michelin was doing things that made no sense at all. The people in sales and marketing were still selling tires on sixty-day payment terms, because that was the common practice in Europe. In order to protect ourselves against supply problems, we had large inventories of raw materials in our factories. But with the runaway inflation in Brazil, the purchase of this inventory entailed extremely heavy interest payments. Michelin had continued to invest money with an eye to the medium and long term, when it should have been reducing its investments to the bare minimum necessary to keep the business running, waiting to achieve a satisfactory cash flow. Price controls were treated as a factor of marginal importance, when in fact they held the key to the success or failure of the enterprise. Responsibility for authorizing price increases had to rest with top management and be subject to weekly review.

Michelin's decision-making processes may have been suitable in a European or American environment, but they were totally inadequate to the situation in Brazil in the mid-1980s.

Furthermore, the company's relations with the government in Brasília weren't good. We didn't have people in place who were capable of making the various administrations understand Michelin's point of view. And our competitors—Firestone, Goodyear, Pirelli—had all been on the scene longer than we had. They hadn't been pleased to see us arrive, and they tried their best to put as many obstacles in our path as possible. But our principal problems were internal, and those were the ones we had to deal with first.

To deal with the debt, the first thing we had to do was to establish a positive cash flow. Second, we had to cut necessary investments to the minimum, reduce our inventories, shorten our customers' terms of payment, and sell any assets that didn't seem indispensable, including all the real estate and buildings that had been acquired when Michelin was gaining a foothold in Brazil but weren't being used anymore. We cleaned house in a big way. My excellent financial director, Philippe Biendel, a top business school graduate, was a great help to me.

We had our share of social problems, as well, including a three-week-long strike at our Campo Grande plant. In a country where inflation was devouring consumer purchasing power on a daily basis, CUT, the principle trade union, had a golden opportunity to rally people to its cause. But during salary negotiations for the renewal of the *convenio*, the annual agreement on employer-employee relations, there was a strike that lasted more than two weeks. The strike began on a Friday, and the picket line blocked access to the factory for the first two days. Now it was imperative that I meet with the manufacturing team so we could take some appropriate steps. On Sunday morning, I called the factory boss and told him, "I'm on my way." He said, "Don't come. They won't let you through." Nonetheless, I got in my car and drove to the factory. When the strikers saw me, they hesitated. The standoff couldn't have lasted more than a minute, but it seemed like a long time to me. And then, probably because I had taken them by surprise, the strikers let me pass. I met with the factory leaders to decide what had to be done. Fortunately, the strike ended in a compromise that was acceptable to everybody.

We had our difficulties in 1986, as the company continued to post losses. But we returned to profitability in 1987 and achieved very positive results in 1988. In 1989, the Brazil operation had a ratio of profits to total sales that made it, in relative terms, Michelin's most profitable division.

During this period, the government of the country moved from one stabilization plan to another, changed finance ministers, and established a new national currency. But inflation continued apace.

We had to steer our way through all those plans and keep the company going at the same time. It required a lot of agility. It was not until the mid-1990s, after the finance minister and future president Fernando Henrique Cardoso instituted a recovery strategy known as the *Real* Plan, that Brazil was able to regain some monetary and financial stability.

I don't think anyone in Clermont-Ferrand ever seriously considered abandoning Brazil, even though we did have to endure a bit of ragging from time to time: "If you don't succeed, we'll have to shut our doors in Brazil." But I was thirty-one, and the notion that I could fail never occurred to me. At that age, you have no doubts. You work day and night if you have to. The moment a problem arises, you deal with it. In 1988, I announced the expansion of the Campo Grande factory, with an investment that increased production capacity by 60%.

All the same, Rita and I had free weekends every now and then, and we went on vacations. And the situation wasn't dire all the time. The tension was at its peak from about the middle of 1985 to the end of 1986; in 1987 things were starting to improve, and by 1988 they were a lot better.

But I wasn't able to enjoy our Brazilian success for very long.

In 1987, François Michelin—who was making his first trip to Brazil—paid me a visit, accompanied by his wife. It was a special moment; this visit allowed me to get to know the man better. We traveled together for about ten days, visiting the factories in Campo Grande and Resende and the plantations in the Mato Grosso and the state of Bahia. Before this, our relationship had been strictly professional.

For companies with operations in every corner of the world, such employer tours were more than a ritual attached to a travel opportunity. Far from wasting time, the Boss made the most of his visit, getting to know the market firsthand and gaining an appreciation of his employees.

François Michelin wanted to get a look at Michelin in Brazil, but he also wanted to get a feeling for the country and get acquainted with its people—that was his biggest reason for coming. People are François Michelin's chief interest. His curiosity was founded on the interest he took in people, whoever they were, from the top to the bottom of the social ladder, without consideration of their age, their origin, or their position in the company. In a certain way, my own career's a testimony to that. When he meets a person, his antennae are up and working. And he's not faking it. Some bosses strike a pose and pretend interest in their employees; François Michelin means it.

In a country where Michelin had become an important foreign investor, the Boss's trip had, of course, its official side. There was a visit to Brasília, the federal capital, to meet José Sarney, the president of the Republic, and his financial minister, Nailson de Nobrega. During our meeting it dawned on us that they knew a lot about Michelin as the producer of the tourists' favorites, the Green Guides, and much less about our main business, the manufacture of tires. We spent considerably more time talking about the Guides, which count for so little in the company's total sales, than about our industrial activities.

When we visited the plant in Campo Grande, we went around to the factory shops and talked with the workers; François Michelin loved doing this. It was a month or two before the negotiations with the unions for the *convenio* were scheduled to begin, and the atmosphere in the factory was a little strange. We went into one of the break rooms, where there were about thirty workers. Their supervisors stayed outside. When the discussion turned to salary conditions, it became quite heated. He didn't back away, and he didn't try to protect himself. He felt he was on familiar ground.

François Michelin has a capacity for astonishment that's rather exceptional. He'd stop at the foot of a tree and ask us questions about its origin, about whether or not it was native to Brazil, about how long ago the species first appeared, and so forth. Most of his questions stumped me, and I had to relay them left and right to get them answered. But he wasn't playing a game; he really wanted to know. I've never met anyone else who's been the head of a large corporation for such a long time who can still look at people and things with such new eyes. And this quality of freshness, of openness, came from the deepest part of him. He's an extremely sensitive man, which explains his respect for other people and their differences, and also explains his curiosity. But he's also a man of enormous experience, accustomed to exercising responsibility. Never mistake his openness for naïveté.

The ten days that François Michelin spent in Brazil turned out to be a defining point for my future career. In a way, his trip was a mutual revelation. That's when I got to know him and he got to know me. A year later, I was transferred to the United States. He must have decided that he knew me well enough to trust me with such a responsibility.

Once again, Rita and I faced a new departure. But my connection with Brazil was now reestablished, having been made even stronger by the arrival of a daughter.

When I left Brazil, I promised my parents that I'd come back to visit them every year, and that I'd bring the kids with me. To this day, I generally spend every Christmas and New Year's Day with my whole family in Brazil.

CHAPTER 5

AMERICA

Another major challenge awaited me in the United States. With its pending purchase of Uniroyal-Goodrich, Michelin was preparing literally to double its size in the world's premier automotive market. On the strategic level, this was a superb move; the timing, however, was not.

I arrived in February 1989, when the negotiations between Michelin and Uniroyal-Goodrich's then-current owner, the New York financial firm of Clayton, Dublier and Rice, were in their final phase. We closed the deal in the beginning of 1990 and began merger operations practically on the eve of a recession. Of course, we didn't know that. Our timing was horrible. The market started to plunge at exactly the same time we started to work on merging the two companies. The purchaser never knows whether or not he's buying at the height of the market— only time will tell. So I had to take charge of Michelin's North American operations, as well as the restructuring of Uniroyal-Goodrich, at a moment when the market was just about to collapse under our feet. Before the purchase of Uniroyal-Goodrich, Michelin North America wasn't doing that badly, but it wasn't doing all that well, either. The head office was certainly expecting better results than what they were getting. Our profits didn't match their expectations.

Above all, Michelin lacked sufficient critical mass to take on Goodyear, which dominated its domestic market. Bridgestone, the number-one Japanese manufacturer, had just taken control of Firestone, a name associated with the automobile industry in the United States since the beginning of the twentieth century.

The tire industry is made up of two markets: "original equipment," that is, the tires purchased by automotive manufacturers for the cars and trucks that come off their assembly lines; and replacement tires, which the owner of a vehicle purchases when his old set of tires is worn out. In North America, Michelin was stronger in original equipment than it was in the replacement tire market. We couldn't have had more than a 10% share of the American market overall. Uniroyal-Goodrich was about the same size as Michelin North America in terms of total sales, but in contrast to Michelin, its strength was in replacement tires. Uniroyal-Goodrich sold tires both under its own brand and under the brands of several other companies. Some of these brands took their names from major department stores or large distribution chains, such as Sears Roebuck or Sam's; others were franchisers who managed national networks. These were known as "associate brands" or "private brands." Blending two enterprises together required a new strategy. We were passing from a single-brand enterprise to a multibrand enterprise.

Uniroyal-Goodrich's industrial equipment was fairly old, and its last owners hadn't invested in it very much. Whenever your business is going through difficult times, you invest as you can, not as you should. Then the moment comes when you can't even manage to achieve the bare minimum. So we had to modernize, reinvest, and downsize.

I decided to close three of Uniroyal-Goodrich's older factories in the United States and Canada. I received a lot of criticism for that. When you launch a difficult operation, you always get criticized. Then, when positive results come in, people applaud and say it was a remarkable accomplishment. It's a common refrain. Businesses have always tried to reduce costs—especially in the United States, where nearly every industry has gone through a cost-cutting phase. I don't see how one can manage a business without keeping one eye glued to expenses. It's a fantasy to think otherwise. Jack Welch, the former CEO of General Electric, was called "Neutron Jack," and Jac Nasser, the ex–CEO of Ford, was nicknamed "Jac the Knife." There have been very few successful extravagant captains of industry.

We had a strategy, but we also paid a lot of attention to the bottom line. If you're managing a business, you can't use your imagination when it comes to costs. You have to be very precise about your debts and your expenses. You need to pay close attention, and if you must take action, you must act energetically. But if that's all you do, you won't get very far.

My second challenge was to put together an executive team from the best people the two companies had to offer. It was a matter of integrating two enterprises that had very, very different cultures. Michelin North America was a thoroughly French outfit. There were some American executives, but the direction was predominantly French. Michelin was a family business, in it for the long haul, chiefly focused on products, quality, investments, and strategy. Uniroyal-Goodrich, because it was formerly owned by a financial firm that specialized in buying and selling corporations, was centered on marketing, on short-term financial performance. It was also a very American company, selling to an American market, while Michelin was established practically everywhere in the world. You couldn't imagine two companies more different culturally.

Michelin's U.S. team remained intact. We took on part of Uniroyal-Goodrich's top management team, but the company acquired a much broader surface. We created so-called "business units," which allowed us to use the majority of the available talent. Uniroyal-Goodrich's CEO left the company, but one of his senior executives took over the business unit responsible for the family cars and vans segment of the tire replacement market. The financial director of the division was a Michelin employee. On the other hand, we coordinated several support functions and put a Uniroyal-Goodrich employee in charge of that. We tried to mix some members of the former Uniroyal-Goodrich team in with the best Michelin people we had. Heads did not roll.

The headquarters of the new corporation was in Greenville, South Carolina, in the offices of Michelin North America. But this did not mean that Akron, Ohio, the rubber capital of the United States, was abandoned; we installed the Uniroyal-Goodrich "business unit" there.

In my new position, I had to apply the lessons I'd learned in Europe and in Brazil, such as cross-manufacturing, with factories specializing in certain products sold under different brand names, and cross-functionality, bringing together executives from different departments—engineering, production, marketing, sales—in order to solve problems collectively from all possible angles.

Another important lesson had to do with managing relations with Michelin headquarters in Clermont-Ferrand. Michelin had much more at stake in North America than it had in Brazil. North America represented 35–40% of Michelin's total sales. As a result, Clermont-Ferrand was much more of a presence among us. The heads of all the big company departments, the financial, legal, commercial, and manufacturing directors, stayed in close contact with the corresponding department heads in the U.S. division. Functional relations like these were important; nonetheless, the head office had to respect the autonomy of the American team. This kind of balance is difficult to achieve. If there's little autonomy, you can't control anything, because you don't know who's responsible for what. Your people say, "The Clermont office told us to do this, so we did it. The consequences were unfortunate, but we're not responsible." You wind up stripping the whole system of responsibility. On the other hand, if you give the North American division too much autonomy, you risk the possibility of developing a Michelin offspring, born inside the company but completely different from its parent organization in

Clermont-Ferrand. The head office was willing to give us some autonomy, but only on the condition that we didn't become too independent.

The corporate environment in the United States bore little resemblance to the situation that confronted Michelin in Brazil. In the United States, it's the market that counts, not the government. In Brazil, our main challenge was the state. Governmental policy had more impact on your profit-and-loss statement than the competition did. In the United States, the market was extremely competitive. "Benchmarking" was a rule of life. We had to take into account the importance of marketing and distribution. Negotiations are more challenging when your customers emphasize high quality, low costs, and long-term payments above all else.

Relations with the major American automakers were difficult, but not more so than elsewhere in the industry. We had discussions about the quantity of tires, about their quality, their technology, and, above all, their price. If you're a supplier, you have to be particularly attentive to your costs and careful in your price negotiations.

It's hard to imagine what a shock it was for the company to move from a single brand name to a multibrand strategy from one day to the next. We made a constant effort to ensure that the solutions we adopted weren't Michelin solutions or Uniroyal-Goodrich solutions but solutions that represented the best choice for this newly created business entity.

The acquisition of Uniroyal-Goodrich gave Michelin a way to get closer to Detroit. Uniroyal was the chief supplier of factory equipment tires to General Motors. The two corporations had a relationship that went back many years. GM was relieved when we arrived, because no automaker wants to be dependent on a supplier that's in financial difficulty. The fact that Michelin was not only prepared to support the Uniroyal brand but also determined to invest in it and develop it was met with great relief. And frankly, the merger would never have come about if GM had been opposed to it. Their agreement had been one of the basic conditions of the deal.

Michelin enjoyed a solid reputation in the United States, where it was known for its technological innovations and the extremely high quality of its products. The automobile manufacturers had a lot of respect for Michelin's products. They thought of Michelin as an enterprise with a lot of resources and a long-term vision. This made us a credible partner. I never encountered the least bit of negativity because I represented a foreign supplier.

Nonetheless, Michelin North America got off to a rocky start. The 1990 U.S. recession, which spread to Europe in 1992, put Michelin's accounts into the red. Between 1990 and 1993, the group accumulated a loss of $1.8 billion. Things were so bad that some observers began to speculate on Michelin's chances of survival. But the company's directors were protected from short-term pressure by the family shareholders and the organization of the company as a limited partnership. This legal structure, a rarity among large corporations, granted virtually discretionary powers to the executives in charge.

We had our difficulties through 1993 and 1994. In 1995, things started getting a lot better. And both 1996 and 1997 were excellent years. After a period of corporate pain, a period that included the merger with Uniroyal-Goodrich, the process of restructuring it, and a slowdown in economic activity, the market recovered and we began to see the results of our merger. We rethought certain habits that had taken root—probably for cultural reasons—in one or the other of the two enterprises, we adopted the best practices of both groups, and that all began to pay off. The year when we really saw the light of a new day was 1995, and things got brighter and brighter in the course of the following years.

Those were perhaps the most important years of my professional education. I had to learn how to be an American CEO, which is much different from being a Brazilian-style boss or a European CEO. For the first time, I was competing directly against our competitors. My education in America was extremely rich: the market, the competition, the mingling of cultures, and the work of restructuring two large corporations, not solely on the basis of costs, but with a view to establishing a new kind of commercial enterprise. The United States is a very good training school for learning about customers, and about everything to do with marketing tools and communication. And it's a school that teaches strict lessons about costs and "affordability." You have to sell your product at a price that people are both willing and able to pay.

I was able to observe the American automobile industry up close, including Toyota, Honda, Nissan, Mitsubishi, and the Europeans and Koreans. And we were not just selling tires to those companies that had assembly plants in the United States or Canada. For example, BMW and Mercedes vehicles arrived in the United States with Michelin tires that were often developed by Michelin North America, built to varying specifications, and shipped to Germany for mounting before the cars' arrival in the United States.

As a supplier, I visited the Nissan factory in Smyrna, Tennessee. I visited the factories of Honda, Toyota, and Ford. The relationship between manufacturer and supplier played an extremely important part in the manufacturer's performance. Every automaker had a distinct personality. The Americans conformed to a certain type, as did the Japanese, but they were by no means all the same. You don't work with Honda the way you work with Nissan or Toyota. They're three different worlds. All three are quite devoted to technological innovation, and they're keenly interested in your equipment. They don't let you manage on your own. They want to know how you're doing things, and when you have a problem, they want to know the cause. They're very meticulous in their dealings with their suppliers. But beyond those common characteristics, you've got three different companies with three very different cultures. And the same thing is true with American car manufacturers. You don't work with General Motors the way you do with Ford or Chrysler. All the same, the three Japanese companies had more in common with each other than they had with the American companies.

Chrysler was a particularly interesting case study. Ever since its founding by Walter P. Chrysler in the mid-1920s, the company had a decidedly tumultuous history, from its dazzling ascent in the 1930s—when, despite the Great Depression, it temporarily replaced Ford as the number-two automaker, behind General Motors—to the long decline that began after the Second World War, interrupted by temporary recoveries. By the beginning of the 1960s, the third of the "Big Three" car companies held less than 10% of the American market. In the 1970s, Chrysler's decision to establish beachheads in Europe with the purchase of Simca in France, Rootes in Great Britain, and Barreiros in Spain ended in financial disaster. In the following decade, the name of the corporation became inextricably linked with that of Lee Iacocca, the man who saved it from ruin.

In 1989, when I went to the United States, Iacocca was still the CEO at Chrysler, but the Iacocca period was nearly over—he retired in 1991. Bob Lutz was the president, François Castaing was the head of the engineering department, and Tom Stallkamp ran purchasing. The whole team that had brought about Chrysler's recovery was still in place.

I was able to draw some important lessons from my encounters with the Chrysler executives. Every year, we'd organize a sort of conference and invite leading people in the industry to speak to an audience of all the top executives of Michelin North America. One year, we invited Bob Lutz to give a talk, and I was struck by the way he discussed Chrysler's problems—he was relaxed, forthright, and crystal clear. He told us, "You know, when we were down at the bottom of the hole, it was fashionable to say that the average intelligence quotient of Chrysler's executives was below 50. Now, since things have started going better, the estimate of our average IQ is above 150. But we've got the same people! The difference is, of course, that our products are more attractive and they're selling better. Before, we were sometimes surprised to find that Chrysler had customers. People bought our products because they could get a good deal, not because the cars were exciting." This very down-to-earth, very relaxed, very modest, very human approach made a deep impression on me. Lying or covering up accomplishes nothing. You have to describe things as they are, and you especially have to describe them clearly, in a way that everyone listening to you can understand.

Another time, Chrysler invited all its suppliers to its newly built research center in Detroit. The reason for the gathering was to say good-bye to Iacocca, who was retiring. François Michelin was sitting at Iacocca's table, and I was at Bob Lutz's. Lutz said to me, "This must be Iacocca's sixth farewell party." I told myself at the time, "When you start thinking about leaving, choose your moment carefully. Go out while you're still on top, not when you're no longer in control of events."

During my time in the United States, the international automobile industry witnessed one of the most bizarre episodes in its history: the Lopez affair.

A native of Spain and a veteran of General Motors' European operations, José Ignacio Lopez de Arriortua was charged by GM with revolutionizing its relations with its suppliers. He was bent on tracking down waste and inefficiency. His rulebook became known by the acronym PICOS: Purchased Input Concept Optimization with Suppliers. In theory, the goal of PICOS was to enroll GM's suppliers in a perpetual cycle of improvement in quality and productivity. In practice, it consisted of reducing the prices GM paid. Lopez was soon nicknamed "the pope of profit."

Revolutionary? Visionary? Mostly, he threw a scare into the industry. What I remember from his project was that it was his, not General Motors'. Apart from the members of his inner circle, who were all Spanish, the people around him didn't support him. When we visited GM factories, the day would always end with drinks and dinner. The people from GM loosened up and spoke quite openly: They'd say things like, "Lopez is causing another crisis," or "Listen to his latest bright idea," or "How dumb is this?" or "PICOS is a crock." When we heard this sort of thing from the mouths of GM executives themselves, we knew it was a bad situation. Suppliers are a little like pupils in a classroom. They don't think about issues any less than their professor, but they don't dare say so. Anyway, inside GM there was strong resentment against Lopez and his Spanish crew. He came over and put on a show, but when all was said and done, the results on the ground always represented a compromise with little resemblance to what he had promised. He did shake up GM, but it was about Lopez, it wasn't about GM. After he left, they took apart everything he'd done.

Lopez left for Volkswagen in 1992. His dramatic exit was followed by a claim of industrial espionage. GM accused Lopez of having taken with him crates of documents. Volkswagen ultimately fired Lopez.

From the outside, it's hard to tell how much he affected GM. Obviously, we had to pay close attention when we negotiated with them. We had some pretty severe clashes with General Motors. But as suppliers, we learned nothing from them. Nothing. Most of all, the Lopez episode worsened relations between GM and its suppliers. If an exercise consists solely in demanding more and more from the supplier, without modifying your relationship with him, that's not going to last long.

It was a lesson that would not be lost on me.

My time in America was a happy one; I really liked living there. When you come from Brazil, and especially from Rio de

Janeiro—an enormous, magnificent city, but violent and unsafe, a place where physical assaults and problems linked to drugs are part of everyday life—and you move into a small town in South Carolina, in the heart of the "Bible Belt," it's night and day. You appreciate Greenville's serenity, its broad avenues, its big houses, its lovely gardens, its charm.

Michelin had been one of the first industries to build a plant in the South. The Southern states were quite eager to industrialize. The unions weren't nearly as strong there as they were in the North, and the labor pool was huge. Michelin likes to go into regions where industrial workers have a strong attachment to the land. They work in the factory, but many of them have a patch of earth they work as well. That guarantees a stable workforce. South Carolina had all these advantages, plus a nearby port in Charleston we could ship out of.

When you arrive in Greenville, people reach out to you right away. An American-style welcome is rather remarkable, particularly in a small town. Social life revolves around institutions— church, school, bridge club, country club, and various children's activities. Parents strongly support their children, not only in their schooling but in their athletic endeavors. To make acquaintances, you don't need to make any special effort. The organized events give you an opportunity to meet all sorts of people. South Carolina was very friendly, very civilized. It was up to you to decide if you wanted a relationship to go further than that. My wife and I still have many friends in the United States.

During this period, our family grew and flourished. It's hard for me to think about the United States without remembering this especially exciting time in my personal life. When we moved to Greenville, we had one daughter, who had been born in Brazil. Three more children were born in the United States. To this day, my children have vivid memories of their years in the States. The "American way of life" is particularly suitable for a young family. We were very happy.

I was quite satisfied professionally as well. My work excited me. I was deeply absorbed by it, but I was able to give it as much as I did only because I had my private space with my wife and my children. I was prepared to stay in the United States a good while longer.

Circumstances, however, would dictate otherwise.

CHAPTER 6

FAREWELL TO MICHELIN

In 1995, Michelin's managers undertook an extensive reorganization of the company. It was the grain of sand that found its way into the machine. They decided that Michelin's structure was too regional—they wanted to make it into a truly global enterprise. They called upon all the principal directors in the company, including me, to come up with ideas about how that goal might be accomplished. How could different synergies be made to work better together? How could interregional management be made less fragmented?

The study was completed at the end of 1995. Early in 1996, Michelin decided to respond to the challenge by reorganizing the company according to product lines: tires for family cars and vans, tires for heavy trucks, farm equipment, and construction vehicles, Michelin maps and guides, and so on. These divisions were going to be operative on a global scale. Geographical zones would support the product lines assigned to them. Functions and specialties were supposed to supply the geographically appropriate product lines in order to strengthen the company's performance.

I was put in charge of perhaps the most important product line, tires for passenger cars and vans. And that was the problem. It was understood that I would stay in the United States, but Michelin merely tolerated this arrangement. It was difficult to direct a complex division that accounted for 40% of the company's total sales from a base in South Carolina. The Michelins were very tolerant and very patient. They didn't tell me to leave the United States. They said, "Stay as long as you must, but remember, at some point you're going to have to come back to Clermont-Ferrand."

.   .   .

This provoked a series of discussions in our family about the future. Major decisions always start with something very practical. My wife, Rita, had no desire to leave the United States. But if we had to leave, she had even less desire to relocate to Clermont-Ferrand. Nor did leaving South Carolina for the capital of the Auvergne seem like a great career move, either.

The restructuring plan seemed to me like a risk for the company. I thought it could pay off, but my own personal situation was a concern. As CEO of Michelin North America, I had a great deal of autonomy; I could fulfill my role in the company while at the same time adding my own personal touch. Going back to Clermont-Ferrand posed a classic problem: You'd always rather be a pastor in a village than a bishop in Rome.

I was forty-two years old, very young to be so near the top. The problem, as I knew well, was that the summit itself would remain unattainable. In accordance with family tradition, François Michelin had picked a Michelin as his successor: Édouard, the youngest of his sons. I knew Édouard well. Early in 1993, François Michelin told me, "I'd like Édouard to go to the United States and work in the North American division for a while." People knew that one day, sooner or later, one of his sons would start being groomed for the succession. We'd divided North America into several "business units." Édouard came to Greenville as head of Michelin's American factories. He was also assigned to the heavy equipment department as head of its commercial sector. It was a big job. His two areas of responsibility represented a large percentage of our total sales.

Michelin had already demonstrated its readiness to promote young talent. All the same, Édouard Michelin climbed up the ladder of the family corporation quickly.

It was clear that if François Michelin hadn't had confidence in me, he wouldn't have sent his son to work at my side. I understood very well that I had to prepare him without giving him lessons. Since we were conscious that we were sharing in the education of the future head of the company, we let him participate in decisions that weren't strictly in his area of expertise. Everything was open to him. For his part, he played the game perfectly. He never stepped out of his role as head of a business unit. He never tried to take advantage of his position, even though everyone knew that sooner or later he was going to become the head of the company. Everything went very smoothly. During the course of two years, we never had a dispute. Early in 1995, Édouard returned to Clermont-Ferrand.

. . .

In 1996, as I was beginning to travel continually, back and forth between the United States and France several times a month, my wife started asking, "What do you want to do? You're forty-two. Are you going to play second fiddle all your life?" She gave a pretty fair assessment of the situation: "You're François's man, and whatever happens, you'll always be Édouard's father's man. And then one day, sooner or later, the time will come for them to turn the page. It's all over." She pointed out that the merger had been completed successfully, that Michelin was making money in the United States, and that I had nothing more to prove.

Personally, I wasn't too bothered by the knowledge that I could never be number one at Michelin. In a family company, that's how legitimacy is passed down. Look at what happened with Ford. When you join an outfit owned and run by a family, family control can't be a surprise to you. Otherwise, you should have gone elsewhere—there are lots of non-family-owned companies. An ambitious person who joins Peugeot, for example, has to take the risk that one day the Peugeot family will consider one of their own competent enough to retake control of the business. It's the shareholders who decide. The Ford family passed the baton, so to speak, and then ten years later they were back in control. This is an element that has to be factored into the equation. Obviously, the probability that a family member is going to be the head of the corporation is generally pretty high. In Michelin's case, I'd say that probability was about 100%.

Then, in April 1996, a headhunter from a big international agency, a Polytechnique alumnus I'd met years before, called. He said, "Does the automobile industry interest you?" I had to laugh. "Of course," I said.

Over dinner together in Paris, the headhunter told me, "Louis Schweitzer at Renault is looking for a second-in-command, someone with the potential to succeed him one day. He's looking at a number of candidates, but I very much want him to make your acquaintance. May I set up a meeting?"

I went back to the United States and talked it over with my wife. She said, "You've got nothing to lose." So I called up the headhunter and gave him the go-ahead. He set up my first meeting with Louis Schweitzer for 8 o'clock in the morning, in his Billancourt office. We passed an hour and a quarter together, talking about Renault. He explained what he was looking for and had me talk about myself. Then he told me, "I'd like you to meet someone." And he brought in Philippe Gras, the man I would presumably replace. After another fifteen minutes, we bade one another farewell and I left.

Two days later, the headhunter called again. "He's very interested, seriously interested. You're now the leading candidate."

Things started to move quickly.

I had a second meeting with Louis Schweitzer to discuss conditions and timing. At the end of July, the CEG, the executive council of the Michelin group, held a work seminar somewhere in the country. I had to call Louis Schweitzer during the seminar to give him my final answer. I had decided to accept his offer. He insisted on fixing a date. I wanted to wait until the end of the year, but he told me, "No, you must come sooner." When the seminar was over, I requested a meeting with François Michelin. He was clearly surprised at what I had to say, but he remained very controlled, very calm. He told me to tell Édouard, so before I left I had a private conversation with him. Édouard was much more positive. He said, "I understand. In the automobile business, that's an offer you can't refuse. But how are we ever going to replace you?" With François Michelin, the emotional level had obviously been higher. He knew that my coming to tell him my decision in person meant that I had thought it through carefully. Did he understand my reasoning? I don't know. But I told him clearly that it would be better for Michelin and probably better for me if I left without much delay.

The fact that Michelin has become a multinational company is due in large part to François Michelin's personality. His business is made in his image. His personal priorities have become those of the corporation, and they've shaped its culture. That insistence on paying attention to individual people, the importance of product quality, the long-term vision, the devotion to the customer, particularly the big automakers—all that comes from him. He *lives* them; they are the foundations of his enterprise. You can't be "Michelin" without being extremely attentive to customers and without focusing hard on technology and product quality. His attitude toward innovation was philosophical: Peculiar ideas were important, because they might contain the key to the future. And it's true—the piece that doesn't fit is the source of innovation. All scientific innovation flows from that. You zoom in on an anomaly and you discover another world. But what counted the most in François Michelin's eyes was the long term. At that time, it was the Japanese who were particularly invested in long-term planning. They were capable of going into new markets and losing money there for years, all the while putting down roots. Only after that had been accomplished would they start trying to optimize their results. François Michelin was convinced that only a long-term strategy could beat the Japanese, a strategy based on products and quality. As long as I've known him—since 1981—he's always considered Bridgestone his most formidable competitor. From the beginning, he's believed that the Japanese tire industry is Michelin's real rival.

In September 1996, at a meeting of Michelin's CEG, I officially said good-bye to the company.

CHAPTER 7

RENAULT

What was it that attracted me to Renault? Cars, to begin with. What's fascinating about the automobile industry is that it doesn't produce an ordinary product. An automobile is the object of both reason and emotion. You choose a car according to certain standards—having to do with quality, of course, and price, and availability—but also according to its image, its design, the sensation it produces. You make a purchase that's rational and emotional at the same time. Few products arouse as much passion as the automobile. It is a love affair that goes well beyond a simple means of conveyance.

Automobile manufacturers are architects more than anything else. They work with people across a vast range of trades and professions. First, you've got the engineers. And the engineering department has different subdepartments: mechanical engineers, electrical engineers, chemical engineers, experts in materials, a whole spectrum of specialists. Then you've got all the people who clothe the engines, the ones who give the vehicles their shapes, their colors, their style. Farther down the line, you've got the marketing people, the salespeople, the financial specialists.

Because the automobile is a part of daily life, the automotive industry interacts with the outside world in a way that many other great manufacturing companies do not. And the workforce is huge: Each of the big carmakers employs hundreds of thousands of people.

For over a hundred years, the history of the automobile industry has been marked by brilliant successes and spectacular failures. For every famous make of car that succeeded in the market during the twentieth century, there have been several that disappeared entirely or became a simple model designation in the sales catalogue of one or another of the industry giants.

There are multiple challenges. And you're never sure whether you've reached sufficiently high performance levels. Many factors go into the customer's choice of a vehicle. You have to pay attention to the brand image, to the interior and exterior design of your products, to everything that has to do with advertising, but also to quality, to how the car will perform in three months, in three years, in five years. Availability is also crucial. And the price has to be calculated with extreme care. So there's this abundance of challenges, and you're never certain that you've responded to them appropriately, because there's always a competitor overtaking you from behind, trying to pass you by. You have to be constantly on the alert; your situation is characterized by permanent uncertainty.

Our history is punctuated with reversals and surprises, and I think that's all due to the fact that the automobile is such a complex object. If you want outstanding success in this market, you have to be good in every area. At a given time, you may attain that level of mastery, but you can never be certain that it will last. That's why changes in management are very risky even though they're often indispensable. There are several examples of a situation where one company or another reaches the top only to find itself in a crisis two years later. But that's what makes this industry so interesting. There are no foregone conclusions, and the game's never over.

My second reason for signing on with Renault was the challenge it presented. In joining a team that was facing difficulties, I saw a chance to make a contribution and to help make a difference. Coming on board during a difficult period is much more promising than hiring on when everything's going well. You can make your mark by contributing to the company in a time of need, and not just because you've been appointed by so-and-so.

I was joining a company where there were no limits. There wasn't any "glass ceiling" for me to bump up against. This was new to me; I was used to working for a company where my possibilities for advancement were finite. At Renault, not only were there no limits but it was clear—as Louis Schweitzer himself had indicated to me—that I would be his successor if things worked out. At that time, he'd been the CEO only since 1992, a little more than three years. But I wasn't in a desperate hurry to get to the top. When I joined, I was forty-two years old. At that age, you don't tell yourself, "I'll be the CEO within two years." What I principally had in mind was to educate myself, to learn a whole assortment of new things. But for the first time, I was signing on with a company where my prospects were unlimited and my path lay open before me.

Renault was founded by Louis Renault in a modest garage in Boulogne-Billancourt, a suburb just outside the gates of Paris, at the end of the nineteenth century. At the end of World War II, the French government nationalized Renault because of its founder's collaboration with the German occupiers. The resulting company, the Régie Nationale des Usines Renault ("State-Owned Renault Factories"), or RNUR, became the symbol of state involvement in industry, an involvement that would soon be the norm almost everywhere in Europe. The RNUR's little cars, which embodied the democratization of the automobile, soon established themselves in the French market and even achieved success outside of France. The 4 CV was produced by a licensee in Japan, where it figured largely in the country's fleets of taxicabs. The Renault Dauphine made a spectacular but ephemeral showing in the United States. The 4 L, a bestseller in the worldwide automobile market, appealed as much to the student in Paris as it did to the farmer in the provinces. The R 5, launched with a particularly innovative advertising campaign, revolutionized the very concept of the compact car. But the RNUR's sole shareholder, the French State, was less concerned with business profits than with social peace. In 1984, it had to make out an enormous check on behalf of Renault to cover the heaviest losses—12.5 billion francs—ever sustained by a French company. First Georges Besse and then Raymond Lévy, ironfisted managers, were called upon to rescue the enterprise. The recovery plan authorized the partial privatization of the corporation, which was renamed Renault SA. But it remained fragile. The quality of Renault's products was not always reliable. Many of its industrial assets were outdated, and its workforce was aging and insufficiently qualified. In 1996, Renault suffered a relapse.

Although Renault had barely recovered from a painful setback—the failure of its merger with the Swedish company Volvo—it had decided to set its sights on other horizons. It was about to start operations in Brazil, in the Mercosur, a region that I know well and have personal ties to.

Louis Schweitzer has a well-deserved reputation as a respected, straight-shooting CEO, but over and above that, he impressed me as someone to whom I could entrust my future. Someone who does what he says. It was very important to me to be able to trust someone in that way.

I joined Renault in October 1996 as executive vice president in charge of purchasing, research, engineering and development, and manufacturing, as well as Renault's efforts in Brazil. I had two months to make a tour of the company and arrive at an analysis and evaluation of its strengths and weaknesses.

People had warned me that I was taking a chance. Executives brought in from the outside haven't always done well at Renault. I was coming from Michelin's United States subsidiary. I'd never worked in Paris during the time I'd spent in France. Renault was a company very much centered on Paris. It was just emerging from state control, and a good number of its top executives had started off as civil servants. So I was something of a black sheep. I had a multicultural past and experience on several continents. But I was exceptionally well received, which is fairly extraordinary at Renault, and the quality of my reception was all the more remarkable since I was starting off very high up in the organization. That gave me an idea of the company's potential and exceptional generosity.

The company was organized into completely separate departments, like silos. The heads of the departments often turned them into baronies or fiefdoms. This was an enormous problem, because I felt the road to recovery lay in implementing cross-functionality. And advocating cross-functionality is tantamount to challenging certain practices that belong to certain functions. But I believed that cross-functionality was fundamental to our success. Fortunately, Louis Schweitzer was very supportive. We had to break down some high walls and reorganize the company so that everyone worked together.

The second difficulty was employee morale. We were dealing with a company that still bore the scars of its recent failures on the international stage. First there was Renault's setback in North America.

European automotive manufacturers had always dreamed of breaking into the North American market; realizing this dream, however, proved extremely difficult. There had been a few commercial successes. But few European car companies had been able to establish a lasting presence the way the Japanese had.

When Renault bought American Motors, the fourth-largest U.S. carmaker, Renault's CEO at the time, Bernard Hanon, believed he had gained a foothold in the United States. But aside from its popular Jeep, the descendant of the rugged machines that had transported American GIs in every theater of operations during the Second World War, AMC didn't have very much to offer. The "Americanization" of Renault's midsized sedans, which had been conceived for the European market, turned into a commercial fiasco. Faced with increasing financial losses, CEO Raymond Lévy decided to throw in the towel. Chrysler picked up AMC for a song. Their Jeep Cherokee models would become a brilliant success a few years later, creating a whole new category called the SUV, or sports utility vehicle. It was a humiliating retreat for Renault.

The company next bet on a projected merger with Volvo, whose charismatic CEO, Pehr Gyllenhammar, was convinced that its passenger car division could no longer maintain the critical size indispensable to its survival. On paper, it looked like an excellent match, a marriage between Scandinavian gravity and Latin charm, between Northern Europe and Southern Europe, between big sedans—worthy rivals of the stately German cars—and zippy compacts. But blunders on both sides, national sensitivities, and the activism of the French government, which still owned more than 80% of Renault's stock, doomed the merger.

So Renault had suffered two reversals, one after the other. A kind of cynicism had set in, the conviction that Renault just didn't know how to do that sort of thing. We had to give people their confidence back. We'd failed twice already. We had to convince our employees and the outside world that success was still achievable.

Renault is a company where people talk things through a great deal. I sat through some interminable meetings where we had discussions about everything and nothing, about tiny details, without any sense of priorities or of what action to take. But once the problem was debated to death and a solution agreed on, the execution, the actual application of the remedy, was often glossed over in a few minutes. A sort of premium was given to fine phrases and arcane knowledge, as opposed to action and implementation. But execution is everything in our industry. I was surprised to see people who lived in the pressure cooker of the automobile business pay so little attention to things I thought were obvious. There was a rhetorical tradition, a love of words, that became more and more pronounced the higher you rose in the hierarchy. People seemed to consider taking action less important than exchanging ideas. They were practically snobs about knowledge. They were impressed if someone knew that such and such a material liquefied at such and such a temperature. There was a sort of affectation in displaying one's knowledge and in engaging in debates that bore no relation to anything that had to be done.

Renault is also a very centralized company. It is controlled, at every level, by the head of the division or company. Whatever the boss says, you do, even if you don't really agree with it. People don't debate decisions very long before they're taken, but they dispute them at length afterward, which is quite detrimental. Everything was organized into distinct sectors, managed by people who claimed to be working together as a team, but who bared their teeth whenever they were challenged to actually cooperate. There was a widespread propensity to resort to excuses for the fact that things weren't going well, rather than to get down to doing what had to be done to make them right.

There were, of course, some bright spots, explaining why this hundred-year-old enterprise, with its troubled past, still belonged to the top echelon of automakers and was still capable of producing surprises. Renault is a company capable of mobilizing very quickly. At bottom, it's a very generous company, with typical French generosity and typically Gallic traits, generous and cynical at the same time. It's bureaucratic but capable of showing great passion for great causes. It doesn't do so well at everyday routine. What the "Renaults" love are grand adventures. It's a company that dares to do things. It's got boldness, creativity, and innovativeness. It's shown more than once that it's capable of passion and conquest. Renault's got all these traits, all these good qualities, helping to protect it.

The only way to become fully integrated into a company with a strong personality like Renault, where the culture can harshly reject you or form a strong attachment, is to make a significant contribution straightaway, to do something those around you can recognize and measure. When I officially took over my duties in December, I went into action at once.

Early in 1996, Louis Schweitzer had declared, "Our cars are too expensive." When he recruited me, Renault had already set itself the goal of reducing its "factory cost" by an average of 3,000 francs (about $600) on every vehicle manufactured.

When I came on, the 3,000-franc plan was just being adopted. I proposed to Louis Schweitzer that we go farther, as long as we could avoid compromising our investments in technology and quality. The 20 Billion Plan, which we announced three months later, in March 1997, was actually just an amplification of that initial project. Renault's recovery plan had a number of components, but its principal one was cost reduction, which was entrusted to me. I contributed very quickly and set a fast pace, taking action, assigning responsibilities, and setting deadlines. People said to one another, "The new guy wants to get things moving."

To my knowledge, there were no personal conflicts, because by definition I'm not a confrontational man. I try to manage pressure when I find it. I don't make scenes or attack people. I'm firm, but not confrontational. When you've come out of nowhere and have landed in such a position in the hierarchy, you don't generally expect much sympathy or cooperation. And you have to expect that everyone will be after your hide if something goes wrong. But I didn't provide very many opportunities for bloodletting. Maybe there were some crises behind my back, but I'm not aware of them. Some people were friendly and others hostile in ways that came as no surprise. Not everyone was pleased with a new second-in-command who didn't know the auto industry, who'd come to Renault from Michelin, from the United States, and who had a rather multinational air to boot. I wasn't born yesterday. Of course, I noticed that a good number of people were not pleased. Nevertheless, in the beginning, I was given the benefit of the doubt. They opted to wait and see what "the new guy" could do. Then, as the plan made progress and the results started coming in, the results silenced the skeptics. People said, "We're about to pull off something we've never been able to do successfully before."

My goal was to knock down the company's internal walls and lay out a set of specific goals and a calendar and stick to them. When I put my team together, I called on men and women who had long experience with Renault and profound knowledge of the company. Some of them later left Renault—Philippe Chauvel and Philippe Ventre, for example, the heads of the engineering departments. But there were also some younger executives on the team, as well as some of the top people in production. They all had in common a deep devotion to the company but were perfectly capable of stern criticism. The team I assembled was made up of remarkable people. They carried out the 20 Billion Plan quite energetically, and in so doing they called into question some habits and traditions that went way back. There was some friction, but never a blowup. The first step was simple: After assembling the team, we established a policy of monthly meetings, days on which we'd review all the problems, create some team spirit, discuss the plan, prepare to put it into action, and "brainstorm" over the results. And since it was clear to me that people were finding it difficult to work together, we set up cross-functional teams. Most of their members were drawn from my areas of competence, but some extended into other departments. In the beginning, the others were a little shy about participating—the great barons of Renault's fiefdoms were suspicious. The rest—research, development, engineering, manufacturing, purchasing, and program directors—were under my responsibility. The other sectors sort of tiptoed along, taking tiny steps forward, and I had to apply a good deal of persuasion, backed up by Louis Schweitzer. He avoided outright conflict but pushed things to the limit.

In the course of the meeting, in which I first estimated the potential savings from our recovery plan at 20 billion francs, I remember quite clearly that someone said, "You must have put in an extra zero by mistake. You mean two billion." They thought my number was hugely exaggerated. At the time, Renault was selling 2.1 or 2.2 million vehicles annually. Cutting costs by 20 billion francs meant a reduction of from 9,000 to 10,000 francs per car in three years.

Some people said, "He's off the deep end. He's raving mad. Doesn't he know that at Renault you set the most conservative goals possible so you can be certain to reach them?" My answer to that sort of thinking was "You're going to get what you ask for. If you set the bar too low, you'll get a low-level performance. But if you put the bar higher, you've got a chance of getting better results." They thought I was clueless. Not only was I going to go down, they thought, I was going to crash and burn. There was a lot of skepticism at every level. Even people very close to me wondered if we were being prudent.

My next step was to sell the plan to the CEO. When I went to see Louis Schweitzer, he asked me if I was perfectly aware of what I was doing. I said, "Yes, I am, and we'll be 20 billion to the good." He said, "The idea is not to reach 80% of the goal, it's to reach 100%, right?" I replied that that was my intention, and he said, "Go for it."

The plan called for cost reductions in practically every area: purchases, factories, research and development, general and administrative expenses, data processing. We went over everything with a fine-tooth comb, but especially purchases, because that was the crux of the matter. And that became my area of responsibility. We called our suppliers together for a meeting, which took place in April 1997. We told them, "For our part, here's what we're going to do in our factories, in our engineering, in our research department. You're not the only ones being asked to make an effort."

The fact that I had worked for a supplier added a great deal of credibility to my arguments. People said, "He worked as a supplier for eighteen years. Where relations with suppliers are concerned, he knows what he's talking about." We presented them with simplified, standardized specifications. We did everything possible to help the suppliers who stayed with us to deal with our cost reductions. We encouraged them to take steps that would help keep them profitable and allow them to benefit from the increases in volume. In the end, everything turned out fine. We had no crisis with the suppliers. They decided to trust us.

Such was not the case with public opinion, which focused on the decision, announced in March 1997, to close the Renault plant in Vilvoorde, Belgium, where more than 3,000 people were employed.

We did an analysis of Renault's production capacities, and it plainly showed that we had at least one factory too many. At least. It would have been easy for us to press harder and find more than one. I'd looked through Renault's records, and I knew that an analysis done long before my time had previously pointed out the Vilvoorde problem. We set up a seminar with Renault's directors. At the meeting, I explained the necessity of simplifying the company's industrial assets, increasing the utilization rate of our existing facilities, and moving toward a system of intensive utilization, where two or three teams would use every asset. This system completely altered the company's conception of its industrial assets. The key element was the number of cost reductions that resulted from this rationalization. Everything pointed to closing the plant in Vilvoorde. It wasn't the most aggressive measure we could have taken. In fact, it was quite reasonable. The decision that was made was in keeping with the logic of the industry. We had to make Renault's prices more competitive.

In Belgium, the announcement of the Vilvoorde plant closing elicited a popular outcry, accompanied by strikes and demonstrations. The situation made the front pages of the newspapers and provoked a storm of social and political protest.

Some people claimed that the reason the reaction to the Vilvoorde closing was so strong was that we hadn't sufficiently prepared people and that the announcement of the decision to shut the plant down came like a bolt from the blue. It was true that Renault hadn't talked a lot about its problems in the past. As a matter of fact, it was Vilvoorde that made people aware, all of a sudden, that Renault had a problem. But there was a simple reason why the news about Vilvoorde came out before we announced the 20 Billion Plan. Louis Schweitzer wanted to prepare the Belgian government by going to Belgium and communicating the decision to the prime minister personally. The prime minister was the one who said it was out of the question and then made the matter public. No one was ready to hear that Renault was in bad shape. When a corporation is going through a difficult period like that and the bad news is constant, people can be brought, slowly but surely, to recognize the facts. That was the case later with Nissan. You can illustrate the difference between the Renault and Nissan recovery plans in this way: When we came up with the 20 Billion Plan at Renault, everyone was surprised. Renault had made money in 1995, and the heavy losses of 1996 hadn't been announced yet. At Nissan, no one was surprised, because people had seen trouble coming for ten years. It's extremely important to prepare the ground, to put all the facts out in the open.

But the closing of Vilvoorde also struck at the heart of a social model long associated with the name of Renault, despite its recent partial privatization and the profound changes that had been under way since the mid-1980s. The affair was a revelation to me.

I'd been in France for five months and in my new position for three. As everyone knew, Renault was a peculiar case—our name wasn't like any other name in French industry. Many people took what we did as a kind of provocation. For decades, Renault had been regarded more as a social laboratory than as an industrial corporation whose chief purpose was to make profits. From the violent social upheavals in 1947 to the general strike in 1968, the "Workers' Fortress" in Billancourt occupied a unique place in the social mythology of France. In November 1986, a French terrorist group assassinated Georges Besse, the first Renault CEO to break tradition in an attempt to turn Renault into a normal company.

For a long time, Renault had been a bastion of the French Communist Party and the powerful trade unions. By successively introducing the third, fourth, and fifth week of paid vacation, Renault had produced more innovations in employer-employee relations than in automotive technology. And this had left a strong imprint on its corporate culture. When I joined Renault, the "Workers' Fortress" was already a thing of the past. Obviously, there were and are still unions at Renault, but the idea of a company functioning in accordance with union dictates no longer existed. Nevertheless, there were still some vestiges of those days. I visited almost all the plants in the Renault group, and sometimes I came away rather alarmed. It was possible for a factory manager with a detailed knowledge of his plant's ergonomics and the latest reports from all the health and safety committees to have no idea what his costs per manufactured unit were, or what the productivity per vehicle was. All things considered, there was much more interest in managing employer-employee relations than in how to obtain the best performance from the factory. It wasn't that the managers were incompetent; they were under the impression that the duties they'd been asked to perform had more to do with maintaining social peace than with running an efficient factory.

Renault's industrial assets weren't very productive, not because they lacked the potential but because no one at Renault had ever really paid much attention to productivity. There was this widespread notion that you couldn't maintain good employee relations and high productivity at the same time. In fact, the opposite is true: You can be quite attuned to social issues while maintaining high productivity. The factories all worked hard to put our plan into action. For our pacesetter, our "rabbit," we chose the Nissan factory in Sunderland. It was at the time, and remains today, the number-one plant in Europe in terms of productivity. We measured the gaps in productivity between Nissan-Sunderland and the other European automobile factories, and we worked with each Renault plant to help it close the gap. I'm pleased to say that the Renault factories are the ones that have made the most progress in productivity, both collectively and individually. If you look at the results for 2000, for example, and compare them to those in 1996, you'll be struck by the difference. As soon as people understood what the goals were, as soon as they knew what could be done and how, they pitched in. Things calmed down in Vilvoorde. The factory was shut down, but Renault came out of it looking good.

One could argue that the 20 Billion Plan marked the end of a transformation at Renault initiated in the 1980s. In this respect, what was at stake for Louis Schweitzer when he made his decision went far beyond a simple factory closing. It completed Renault's conversion to the principles of capitalism, as illustrated by the resounding approval privatization received in 1996 from the company's own employees.

The process of closing the Vilvoorde factory included a plan to assist the employees affected. Two years after the closing, fewer than 200 of its 3,200 employees had failed to find work.

The Vilvoorde affair earned me a certain notoriety, the nickname *le cost killer.* That reputation would precede me to Japan.

In Europe, and especially in France, employment is a traumatic issue. I watched the difficult years in Europe, 1992 to 1994, from the vantage of the United States, but I know that unemployment monopolized the television news in France. When you're subjected to such an intensive barrage, any unemployment, at any time, can be traumatic. Employment becomes a value in and of itself. I'm not saying that employment isn't important, but people need to understand the conditions of a healthy employment rate, and that isn't always the case. Economic life consists of destruction and creation, of change. It's all part of the normal functioning of an economy. To consider employment as an immutable good is profoundly contrary to the way an economy evolves. When you try to save a job that's been condemned by market evolution or technological progress, all you succeed in doing is weakening the business as a whole.

The success of Renault's 20 Billion Plan surprised even the believers at how fast the company came back to good health. In 1997, the turnaround occurred very quickly; 1998 was even more phenomenal, and we did still better in 1999. That was due to our products, which were selling well, but also to the appreciable reductions in our costs. With the company's recovery, I had earned my stripes. I was now a legitimate member of the Renault family.

CHAPTER 8

LOOKING FOR

ACQUISITIONS

On May 7, 1998, in London, Daimler's CEO, Jürgen Schrempp, and his counterpart at Chrysler, Bob Eaton, announced a "merger between equals" that gave birth to a new giant in the automotive industry: a company of 440,000 employees, $155 billion in annual sales, factories in 34 countries, a catalogue ranging from Mercedes to Jeep, a capitalization valued at close to $100 billion. The new giant joined GM and Ford as the top three carmakers in the world.

The Daimler-Chrysler merger caused a shock wave in the automotive world. "If those two companies are joining together, what's going to become of us?" we thought.

All of a sudden, Renault felt very small. DaimlerChrysler was twice the size of Volkswagen, the number-one carmaker in Europe. The analysts predicted that only automotive manufacturers capable of building at least 4 million vehicles a year would survive in the global market.

At a meeting of the corporate executive committee, Louis Schweitzer said, "We have to give serious thought to an alliance with another carmaker."

We skimmed through the possibilities. We tossed out Ford and GM, because they wouldn't have resulted in the balanced alliance we had in mind. Some people said, "Why not try again with

Volvo?" But our hearts weren't in it. Fiat in Italy wasn't right either. Rover had already come under the control of BMW, and things weren't going very well. The choices came down to two Japanese companies, Nissan and Mitsubishi, and one Korean company.

A team headed by Georges Douin, Renault's chief of international affairs, was charged with analyzing its possible partners in the Far East.

I stated my position from the start: Any alliance, whatever its terms, costs a great deal of effort. Whether the partner is big or little, a merger offers the same order of difficulty. If we're going to form an alliance with another company, let's aim high and pick the biggest partner. It was plain to me that our choice should be Nissan. I'd had some rather discouraging experiences with Korean carmakers when I was in the United States. They seemed very sure of themselves, drawing up highly ambitious plans that were never realized. The Japanese seemed much more reliable.

Nissan, the number-two Japanese carmaker, had exhausted its resources in a vain effort to keep up with the leader, Toyota. For Nissan, as for the Japanese economy generally, the 1990s were a "lost decade." During this period, with the sole exception of 1996, Nissan posted a string of annual deficits. The company needed money, fast. It seemed possible that the end of fiscal year 1998 (March 31, 1999) might push Nissan into insolvency or force it to seek help from the Japanese government. Courageously, the president of Nissan, Yoshikazu Hanawa, made the rounds of the industry's stalwarts, looking for a white knight. Ford declined. Renault initiated contact with Nissan, and since the fall of 1998, negotiators and technicians from the two companies had carried on cordial, productive discussions.

By January-February 1999, DaimlerChrysler and Renault were the only two contenders left. We knew that if Daimler-Chrysler wanted to make the deal, they'd be the favorites. They'd just completed the merger between Daimler and Chrysler. The press produced a stream of articles praising them for their superb strategy, which had radically altered the competitive landscape of the automobile industry. They offered a range of famous makes, they were established all over the world, and they had plenty of money. And no one could ignore the prestige that Mercedes enjoyed in Japan. For all these reasons, we thought of ourselves as the challenger, the underdog. It was clear that DaimlerChrysler, if it wanted to, had a much better chance than Renault to carry the day.

But we persevered, because we couldn't ignore how complementary our two companies were, and we had a vision of the synergies that would result from an alliance. Our contacts with the Nissan people had been sufficiently satisfactory to make us think it was worthwhile to stay the course.

In March 1999, while I was at the Geneva International Motor Show looking at the exhibits, a colleague from Renault found me and told me, "We just learned that DaimlerChrysler has withdrawn." The Germans' DaimlerChrysler board of directors, starting with Schrempp, had tended to be in favor of seizing this unique chance, but the Americans had opposed it ferociously. All at once we realized that we were alone in the race. Up until it withdrew its offer, DaimlerChrysler had given no sign whatsoever of flagging interest, so the announcement of the withdrawal was a shock. Since we'd considered ourselves as the challengers and the prospect of reaching an agreement had seemed so unlikely, we were completely unprepared psychologically for this turn of events. Before this, Renault's efforts toward forming an alliance had elicited little response inside the company. There were lots of people involved in the discussions, but they did their work without really daring to believe it might lead to anything. After the failed union with Volvo and the retreat from the United States, we didn't want to be disappointed for the third time.

Nissan's managers had had the prudence or the prescience to keep both irons in the fire and had never broken off the dialogue with Renault, even when it appeared DaimlerChrysler would be the winner. I wasn't directly involved in the discussions between the Renault and Nissan teams. But I told Louis Schweitzer I'd give him a hand if he needed me. The result was that I presented Renault's 20 Billion Plan to Hanawa and Nissan's top executives back in November. Hanawa was impressed enough that he asked Louis Schweitzer to send me to Japan if their two companies reached an agreement.

Renault's negotiators were pushing for a kind of subsidiary arrangement, a joint venture, and the Japanese would have none of it. I stepped in and proposed that we set aside the legal structures and do something much more informal: set up cross-company teams, or CCTs. I went back to Tokyo in December 1998 to give more details about the CCTs and explain how they worked. This and my 20 Billion presentation were my two contributions to furthering the negotiations.

DaimlerChrysler's withdrawal dramatically simplified the choices before Nissan's executives: It was either Renault or nothing at all. But Louis Schweitzer refused to take advantage of the situation to renegotiate the terms he'd offered: Renault had offered to purchase 36.8% of Nissan's capital for $5 billion, and the two corporations would form an alliance. Each partner would retain its identity and its brand names.

Immediately after the DaimlerChrysler announcement, Louis Schweitzer asked to see me. He told me, "You must be aware that I have only one person in mind who can go to Japan and do this job, and that person is you." Was I surprised? No. Considering my record, it seemed to be the next logical step. I'd always thought someone would have to go to Japan if we made the deal. And being as objective as possible under the circumstances, I thought that if I were in Louis Schweitzer's place, I'd have chosen me, too. I wouldn't pick a person who'd never lived abroad, who had no experience in restructuring a company, who'd never demonstrated an ability to work in a different culture than his own, and send him into such a situation. I had the "ideal" background. But I thought through all these things without really believing that any of them would ever come to pass. On the other hand, when I learned that DaimlerChrysler had pulled out, I was pretty sure that I would be on my way to Tokyo. In a manner of speaking, it was the decision I'd hoped for. From the start, I was all for choosing Nissan. I'd argued at length in favor of them, and I was aware that I was probably the person best qualified to accept the challenge Nissan presented. I could hardly defend my conviction that Nissan was our best option without agreeing that we had to send our best-qualified executive to do the job.

In fact, Louis Schweitzer declared that he would cancel the alliance if I refused to go. Schweitzer was quite clear about that. He told me, "I've got only one candidate for this job. And that means that if you won't go, I won't sign." I told him that I understood but that it was more than my decision alone—I'd have to consult my family. My wife and four children had been in France barely two years. To move to a completely unknown country wouldn't be easy for them. On a professional level, I was ready. I knew that nobody at Renault was as well prepared for the task as I was. Deep inside, I felt that this was the reason I'd joined Renault. This was the moment my whole career had prepared me for. It seemed right and logical. But I had to persuade my wife. As it turned out, persuading her wasn't all that difficult. She understood that this was an uncommon challenge. She said, "It's an extraordinary opportunity, and I know you're going to make a success out of it. It'll open up prospects for you that you've never even dreamed of. It's going to be difficult, but it's the professional chance of a lifetime. We have to go." I was the one who was a little uneasy. We'd recently bought and restored a house. Now, after we've been living in it for barely three months, I come in and announce that we're leaving for Japan. Despite what she said, it was hard on her.

Nissan was Louis Schweitzer's decision. Frankly, even if there had been opposition to the scheme among Renault's directors, it wouldn't have made much difference. Unanimity was a secondary consideration. There was no vote, no show of hands around the table. You showed where you stood by arguing for or against the proposition. But, at a certain point, Schweitzer cut off discussion and said, "It's Nissan." He didn't hesitate; he moved decisively. The decision to form the Renault-Nissan Alliance was his. He's the one who took the risk. He listened to the others, he listened to me, he even counted on me. But he assumed the responsibility for the choice.

All that remained was to get the go-ahead from Renault's principal shareholder, the French government, which still retained a 44% stake in the company. The government department in charge of public finance, which manages France's participation in state-run or partially privatized companies, was game. The definitive word, however, had to come from Prime Minister Lionel Jospin. The fact that Louis Schweitzer had direct access to him was of great help. And so our chief shareholder endorsed Renault's plan. But the government chose to remain in the background while Renault and Nissan came to terms. In the middle of March 1999, shortly after Schrempp announced DaimlerChrysler's withdrawal, Renault finalized its offer.

On March 27, Louis Schweitzer and Yoshikazu Hanawa unveiled the Renault-Nissan Alliance to the international press at Nissan's Tokyo headquarters in the Keidanren Kaikan. Reactions to the news ranged from astonishment to hostility. Even under the rosiest of prognostications, the operation looked like a leap into the unknown.

I knew it was risky. There were no guarantees that we'd succeed. But this was such an opportunity for Renault that we had to try. It's always easier to appreciate the dimensions of a risk in hindsight. However, the opportunity was so great it made the risk seem negligible, both for Renault and for me personally. One day, just as he was about to sign the agreement, Louis Schweitzer asked me how I estimated my chances of success. I told him, "Fifty-fifty," and then I asked him, "How about you?" He didn't give me a percentage. But he said, "If I'd thought you had only a 50% chance of success, I wouldn't have agreed to the Alliance. I wouldn't have gambled Renault at fifty-fifty." He was more of an optimist than I was.

Among Renault's peers in the automobile industry, the predominant reaction was skepticism. Even in France, the reaction was rather cool, particularly among people in the automobile business. Jacques Calvet, former head of Peugeot Citroën, said, "In my opinion, the drawbacks, the financial risk, the juxtaposition of two product lines more competitive than complementary, and above all the enormous difficulty of making two teams, culturally light-years away from each other, work together, all seemed to outweigh the potential advantages."

By stressing the cultural differences between Renault and Nissan, Calvet astutely put his finger on what would be our greatest challenge: making sure that two cultures, two identities, two personalities could live and work together harmoniously.

Everyone says that DaimlerChrysler missed an excellent opportunity. But I'm not sure they would have made a success of the operation. It's not easy to manage a cultural intersection of this type.

Bob Lutz, well known for his willingness to speak his mind, estimated that carrying out the Nissan operation would be the equivalent, for Renault, of putting $5 billion in a containership and sinking it in the middle of the ocean.

CHAPTER 9

ARRIVING IN JAPAN

My family and I arrived in Japan in May, taking advantage of the school holidays in France.

Renault's team did things right. Philippe Lecomte, the personnel director, contacted a French expert on Japan whose ex-wife was Japanese. She took us on our first tour of the country. While I was working, the children ran around everywhere and everybody pampered them. The whole week we were there, the kids were happy. I was quite struck by this—it was my first surprise. Bringing them to live in Japan was something of a gamble, because I didn't know how they were going to react. But they were delighted with their first contact with the country. They started to learn a few Japanese words. On the weekend, we left the city and spent a few days in a country inn. They had special meals for the kids, who got a sense of the kindness and courtesy of the Japanese people. Children are very sensitive to that sort of thing, and as a result they really enjoyed their first experiences in Japan. At the end of their stay, as they were preparing to leave, they asked me, "Say, Daddy, when do we get to come back to Japan?" It was quite a relief to know that they would be happy in Japan.

My wife was less enthusiastic, because she realized that she couldn't understand anything—anything written, anything that people said. She worried about the house, and the school, and driving in Tokyo. She was worried about how to organize our family life and how long it would take. She knew that work was going to eat up all my time, so she wouldn't be able to count on me very much. She was uneasy about fitting into Japanese society, and she had no idea how much time would have to pass before family life would become normal again. She was experienced in living abroad, but we hadn't liked any of the few houses we'd looked at, and we hadn't been very impressed by the school we visited.

For any Westerner newly arrived in Japan, a visit to a supermarket is a guaranteed culture shock: Tokyo was and remains the most expensive city in the world. Like other wives, Rita had a hard time recovering from the shock of Japanese prices. When you've lived in Brazil and you arrive in Japan and discover that tomatoes are sold in units of one and that a melon can cost as much as $50, well, that's a shock. And when you have a family of four children accustomed to Western eating habits, the cuisine can be a bit disconcerting. The problem wasn't our increased expenses in themselves, because she knew that our income would be adjusted to correspond to the higher cost of living. But paying $50 for a melon when she knew she could buy almost a truckload of melons for the same price in Brazil—that was shocking. During that first week, she came back from the supermarkets completely demoralized.

The language barrier was huge. When you first get to Japan, you're really constrained, because you feel dependent on other people for everything. If you want to talk, you need an interpreter. If you want to go somewhere, you need someone to drive you. The culture's different. The customs are different. Adults find it harder than children do. Kids see everyone being nice, and smiling, and they feel safe, whereas adults have the sensation of going backward, returning to a condition of dependence they haven't known since childhood. As time passed, however, our family got its bearings.

Before I came to work at Nissan, I can't say that I knew the Japanese well. When I was with Michelin North America, we sold tires for factory equipment to Toyota, Honda, and Nissan. What I knew about them was that there was no such thing as a "Japanese carmaker," as I mentioned before. Toyota, Honda, and Nissan were three very different enterprises with three very different cultures. Characterizing a company as "Japanese" doesn't really tell you anything about it.

Honda, for example, was a very technologically oriented company. They were quick to adopt Michelin tires, which supplied most of their factory equipment in the United States. In the case of Toyota, it took us ten years before they would authorize a Michelin tire. But Honda brought us a prototype, and we had to identify suitable tires for it. A debate arose between Honda's engineers and Michelin's. Honda had an industry analyst come over from Japan, who acted as arbitrator. He drove the prototype with several different kinds of tires, and then he said, without even looking, "This is the set of tires I want." The discussion was over. Honda relied on pragmatism, technical excellence, and expertise. Their people were very open-minded when it came to tire brands and very hard-nosed when it came to negotiating prices.

Toyota was a different world. A mighty force in Japan, where it owned 40% of the domestic market, Toyota was imperious and sure of itself. Toyota was slow to venture abroad—Honda and Nissan moved beyond the shores of the archipelago first—but once it did, it advanced like a steamroller. Dealing with Toyota meant dealing with people who were very aloof. They exuded a sense of power. They had a binary vision: On one side, there was their system, and on the other side, the rest of the world.

Compared to Honda and Toyota, Nissan's image was a little hazy. It was a company capable of operating at a high technical level. I'd driven the Infiniti Q45 in the United States and the car had made a big impression on me. I also tried the 300ZX, which was a wonderful automobile. But alongside those, we saw some things come off the line that we couldn't make heads or tails of. Nissan's corporate personality was confused. It gave the impression of an amalgamation of elements piled up on top of one another without anything resembling a strategy.

Given these conditions, it was hard for me to understand how people could speak of the Japanese automobile industry as though they were referring to a single whole. They all had, nevertheless, some common characteristics: a taste for technology, a determination to refine and improve the industrial process, and an insistence on quality. The Japanese are a very meticulous people. If they heard that we'd had a manufacturing accident, they'd want to see the machine it happened on and they'd want to know under what conditions the accident occurred. They put a lot of effort into learning about the details of our everyday operations. If they were trying to find the origin of a problem, they'd go look at an extruder to see how you were drawing the tires, what the temperature levels were. The representatives of the American carmakers never made that kind of request. It would never have occurred to them.

And in fact, the Japanese left an indelible mark on the automobile industry by extending the boundaries of the factory management system known as Taylorism. The Toyota Production System (TPS), developed by legendary engineer Taichi Ohno, was a pragmatic approach founded on observations of the workings of an American supermarket. The goal of the TPS was the complete elimination of the wastage—of raw materials, of time, of space—that characterizes heavy industry. It was at Toyota that "lean production" was born. The system would be copied and adapted, more or less successfully, by the automobile industry worldwide, beginning with Toyota's competitors in Japan. Later, the system became public knowledge through a best-selling book, *The Machine That Changed the World*, written by researchers at the Massachusetts Institute of Technology (MIT). The Japanese aren't champions of theory. Their strong suit is to start from a simple, pragmatic observation and to try to create a solution from that. I haven't seen very many theoretical solutions produced in Japan.

. . .

When I walked through the door of Nissan's headquarters in the Ginza district of Tokyo for the first time after the signing of the Alliance, I was the perfect "outsider": foreign to Japan, to its networks, to its conventions, and to its prejudices.

Nissan's headquarters are located in lower Ginza, between Chuo dori, known as "the Champs-Élysées of Tokyo," a broad avenue famous for its shops, and the Tsukiji fish market.

In advance of my first day at Nissan, I'd submitted a list of the things I wanted to see and the meetings I wanted to have. Everything had been organized. At the time, the office that's mine today was the office of Mr. Hanawa, the president of the company. So they put me in a room on the same floor, a huge meeting room crudely converted into an office. I saw that I'd have to do everything over from scratch.

The first person I met was one of the secretaries, who helped me with the usual arrangements—badge, telephone numbers, and so on. Shortly thereafter—in a stroke of luck for me—a young woman was assigned to me as my assistant: Miyuki Takahashi. She's very smart, very lively, and knew Nissan well. She had lived in Europe, in Holland, before working in the North American section of Nissan. Little by little, I built a nucleus of people around me.

When I arrived, the chief reaction among employees was curiosity. They'd already read the newspaper articles. I was preceded by my reputation in the press as "the cost killer." So, of course, I was surrounded by curious people. "Who is this? What can he do for us? What's going to happen? How's he going to go about it?"

I was bound and determined to become assimilated. When I signed on for this Japanese adventure, I told myself that Japan was going to be a part of me, just as Nissan was going to be a part of me. But assimilation doesn't mean that you have to lose your individuality or your originality. And in any case, I knew I'd always be different here. I tried to be myself. I tried to assimilate, but without phoniness. In the end, they saw that I was pretty transparent. There were some moments of pressure, tension, fatigue, but I don't remember ever losing my self-control or exploding in anger, although to tell the truth there were sometimes good, solid reasons for doing so. Even if my impatience bothered people, I was friendly, I was open, I wanted to talk to people and learn things.

The Japanese are very courteous people, sensitive to the feelings of others. They'll never speak to you unpleasantly. When they don't think much of you, they keep quiet. But when they think a lot of you, they tell you so. Even if many of them believed that I wouldn't do the company any good and we weren't going to succeed, they were far too polite ever to say anything to me about that. This Japanese trait helped me to avoid more rows than I could have hoped. I didn't need to hear any speculations on the topic "What have Renault in general and you in particular come to teach Nissan?" There were lots of silent people. I interpreted this silence as neutrality at best and a negative opinion at worst. There weren't a great many people who were very positive right from the beginning. We were facing, at best, widespread skepticism. But in any case, during those first months I was spared harsh criticism and negative comments. This was a big help. I didn't need anyone making my task more difficult.

The Japanese press, thoroughly familiar with the critical situation the Japanese carmaker was in, gave the new Alliance the benefit of the doubt. But a sense of skepticism carried the day in the international press.

Japan's political leaders probably breathed a discreet sigh of relief. The announcement of the Alliance relieved the government of the necessity of facing a grim choice: either to watch a jewel of Japanese industry collapse, or to reach into its own pockets to bail Nissan out. Some officials told me, "We're quite pleased with this alliance. We'll do all we can to make it work." They were delighted to have someone extract a painful thorn from their side, put up some money, and send a management team. If it hadn't been for Renault, they wouldn't have had anyone at all. They were relieved and clearly wanted us to succeed.

As to Nissan's chief Japanese competitors, Toyota and Honda, they saw the Alliance as more of a nuisance than a genuine competitive threat. It was as if a small mosquito had entered their domain. A mosquito is aggravating, it's got an annoying buzz, but in the end a little bite is the worst it can manage. I don't think anyone really took us seriously in the beginning. No one thought we would get very far. The French were flinging $5 billion into a bottomless pit, all the commentaries said. At best, the writers were jaded and condescending. To this day, some of our competitors think we're cooking our books. I know this because several analysts have told me so. Try to imagine what it must have been like in 1999.

I was so occupied with things inside the company that I had neither the time nor the inclination for social engagements outside. People reached out to me and suggested that someday, when I had the time, we could have dinner or drinks together. Some of them were Japanese. Others were foreign suppliers and consultants, people interested in what we were going to do. I received some advice from outside the company, too—advice about what one could and couldn't do in Japan, about exercising the necessary patience. I listened to them, but it was clear to me that what they had to say wouldn't exert a great deal of influence on my decisions. The company was in such a state of deterioration that the solutions to its problems, if any, were going to have to be found on the inside. My plan was to work with my team, devise a certain number of basic principles, and follow them. What other people told me was interesting but not convincing. Every time someone advised me to take my time, to exercise moderation, to be less ambitious, and so forth, the words just went in one ear and out the other. I knew instinctively that this wasn't the direction we had to move in. What we had to do at Nissan was to reawaken passion, reconstruct a vision, rediscover a rhythm, put things back in phase, give the company a project, and deliver the impetus to carry it out. If I had to sum up what was needed, I'd say fire, intensity, and light.

CHAPTER 10

ASSEMBLING A TEAM

ouis Schweitzer told me, "It's up to you to choose your team. It's absolutely indispensable for you to feel confident about the men and women you take with you. I'll advise you, but the choice will be yours, and I'll do everything I can to see that the people you choose are relieved of their current duties and free to go."

Between the end of March and July, we carried out an extensive analysis of Nissan. We looked at certain operations that both companies performed and examined their outcomes so that we could identify which positions required us to send Nissan some Renault people and vice versa.

The first name I put on the list was Patrick Pelata, from Renault's engineering department. Several months before, when we gave that department a thorough reorganization, I'd promoted him to executive in charge of development. Now I needed someone with engineering credentials solid enough to make him credible in the eyes of his new Japanese colleagues. Nissan was famous for its engineering. Our team had to have a certain number of highly qualified technical experts, and Pelata fit the bill. And he was young, open, and dynamic.

To head the enormous finance department, a crucial element in a company burdened by debt, I chose Thierry Moulonguet, a former director of public finance for the French government whom Louis Schweitzer had recruited to become part of

Renault's strong financial team. Investments, purchases, trade in raw materials, cash-flow management, foreign exchange, consumer credit: The automobile industry handles enormous amounts of money, and the difference between a well-managed and a poorly managed treasury can be decisive. For historic and structural reasons, the financial side of the business had been given little consideration in Japanese companies. Moulonguet joined the board of directors as associate financial director and soon took over control of financial operations.

In all I brought thirty people from Renault. All thirty were important, but some were essential. I chose a few of them myself, and I added others because many people recommended them. Pelata and Moulonguet came on board very early and wound up on the board of directors. People like Philippe Klein, Bernard Long, Bernard Rey, and Dominique Thormann were extremely important. Klein assisted me directly, and Rey kept an eye on purchasing. Thormann was responsible for communications. Bernard Long was in charge of human resources, and his responsibilities included the management of our upper-level executives. The success of the enterprise would largely depend on the quality of their work.

The team took shape little by little. It was based on the analyses I was making in Tokyo and the feedback I was getting from the Renault people about what they were discovering. Some were volunteers. We put the team together so quickly and so efficiently because Renault gave us its complete support. Everyone at Renault, without exception, recognized the enormous opportunity Nissan was offering us. And their response was a burst of solidarity and enthusiasm. I had the feeling that people were saying to one another, "We've got to pull together to help Ghosn and his team." I never saw a hint of jealousy of anyone guarding his territory. No one said, "No, I can't let so-and-so go over to Nissan. He's too important to Renault." From the start, they were convinced of their obligation to send me the people I needed and willing to make whatever sacrifice was required. Later, Louis Schweitzer declared quite openly that my project was Renault's strategic priority. Everyone knew we could lose everything in this operation, and they all pitched in. The reaction was unanimous. Recommendations came from everywhere.

Some candidates were so excited by the project that they came to tell me—or they had others tell me—that they were game. This was already a strong argument in their favor, because I wanted people who were enthusiastic about going to Japan. I didn't want them to come under constraint. When they seemed hesitant, I let them off the hook right away. I knew the task was going to be difficult and that we were going to ask a lot of them. My other criterion was that I wanted open-minded people. However competent a candidate may have been, however motivated, if I sensed that he or she was even slightly closed-minded about cultural differences, that person was excluded. I didn't want there to be any chance that one of my people would behave like a colonist. I wanted competent, enthusiastic, open-minded people capable of engaging in a real dialogue. Not one of those who joined the team was forced to do so, and not one was imposed on me in any way. I more or less co-opted every one of them.

It was indispensable that the people who were coming to Nissan should know Renault well. If we had established the first connections between the two companies with people who didn't know Renault, we would have doomed ourselves to failure. I never once thought about signing up someone from outside the company.

Once the list was complete, Renault's management did its best to prepare the members of the team for what was going to be, for the great majority of them, a leap into the unknown. The whole team spent two days together in Paris. The idea was to weld the group together. We had Serge Airaudi, a French expert on Japan, come and talk to us about Japan. He described the country as he saw it. He didn't presume to tell us what we would have to do. He shared his experiences, which were much more interesting and, as it turned out, quite useful. He didn't act like someone who was lecturing us. I was always a little skeptical about the people who tried to hold forth, who said you'd have to do this and that when you got to Japan.

The seminar took on some of the character of a pregame locker-room pep talk. I had told everyone from the start this wasn't going to be any picnic. None of you are going to Japan by accident, I told them; second, you're going to have to be more than 100% motivated, because this is going to be hard. I want coaches, people who can help out, problem solvers, not people who cause problems themselves. We don't have time for that sort of thing.

The team members left France for Japan at intervals all through summer 1999. I came first. I started making round-trips back and forth as soon as the agreement was signed in March. I was still executive vice president of Renault. Pierre-Alain De Smedt, my replacement from the Spanish automaker SEAT, was not slated to arrive until September 1999. Up until June, when I was named chief operating officer of Nissan, I'd spend a week in Tokyo, followed by a week in France. After my appointment, I invested myself totally in Nissan. There was never any passing of the baton between me and De Smedt.

It's something of a shock to find yourself suddenly embedded in a fairly opaque Japanese organization, without an office of your own, unable to speak the language, with all your reference points gone. I knew it was going to be hard. And I also knew it would take a while to establish real ties with Nissan. Some of the Renault people were more successful than others at this, but generally speaking our team's attitude throughout this period was absolutely impeccable. They suffered in silence. And then, little by little, with a bit of help here and there, they managed to get their bearings.

To sustain troop morale, I gather the ex-Renaults together from time to time—once or twice a year—in some discreet off-site location. I never wanted us to give the impression that we were the French clan. If the head of the company is perceived as part of a clan, he loses credibility. The original Renault team did a remarkable job, and it was normal for me to show my appreciation now and then. But I showed it within the framework of company performance. I give a lot of credit to the Nissan team for having rebuilt the company. Without the little nucleus of French expatriates, none of this would have been possible. They performed Herculean labor, making connections, proposing solutions, expressing doubts when they had to. They buzzed through the company like bees. I think that a large part of what's been accomplished here would not have been doable without this team of competent, open-minded, enthusiastic people.

It would have been unrealistic to try to force change on Nissan's culture all at once. That would be deeply contrary to human nature. People who try to impose one system onto another only wind up destroying it. This has never been our strategy. If Renault had wanted to do that, they would have picked anyone but me, because I'm completely convinced of the opposite course. Nissan had to be changed from the inside. If you're French and you come to Japan, you have no chance, zero, of budging the system an inch. I'm convinced of this. My conviction is both human and professional, and it's bolstered by the experience of having lived on several continents. Right from the beginning, I told them: "You're not missionaries. You've come here not to change Japan but to straighten out Nissan with the men and women of Nissan. We're the ones who have to assimilate with them—it's not up to them to adapt to us. Nissan's people are going to revive the company, and we're here to help them." And everything happened in accordance with this strategy. Obviously, some people wanted us to go faster, they wanted us to lay down some rules, but that would have been absolutely wrong, a flagrant error. There were those who were of the opinion that we should have pounded the table more often. But that sort of behavior has never solved any problem. The results show that what has been done wasn't very far from being the only possible approach. A bridge-building approach, founded on reason but on emotion as well, basically oriented toward objective performance and toward restructuring the company. We were not doing this or that to satisfy Renault. We were doing it because, objectively speaking, it would create more wealth for the Renault-Nissan Alliance. It's a long-term approach: You lead a company through its revival, you create wealth, and you give positive reinforcement to the people who contribute to the effort.

CHAPTER 11

ANALYZING THE PATIENT

Our people at Renault had examined Nissan's numbers closely and reported them to me, so I was informed about its financial condition and its balance sheet. But I've never given too much importance to numbers that appear in a document detached from reality. I knew that the company's situation was serious, but I wanted to investigate it from the inside and see what was hiding behind those numbers.

By March 1999, I knew that the company was performing very badly. I'd looked at the books, the past and present results, the net operating profit after taxes, the results posted by the different subsidiaries, and the various segments of the market. The overview I had wasn't exactly dazzling.

From the moment the negotiations began, there were all sorts of people participating in discussions with the Japanese, forming impressions of them and their company. But generally speaking, they were just that—impressions—and not factual, carefully constructed analyses. They were more like news flashes or anecdotes. The picture that resulted from them was quite confused. I didn't put much faith in them. At that stage, I was concentrating on numbers and results, because they translated the reality of the company. But at the same time, I knew we had to treat the data we were given with a certain skepticism. We wondered if we weren't going to find something worse. Did these results depict the true situation? So my image of Nissan was pretty hazy. The company's deterioration was obvious, but I had no idea about the real cause of that deterioration. I suspected management problems, strategic problems, problems involving imprecision and lack of coordination, but I didn't have a clearer idea than that.

On paper, Nissan was in a critical state. Its domestic market share had been in decline for twenty-seven years in a row. In the eighties, Nissan had run just slightly behind Japan's leading car-maker, Toyota. But now Nissan's sales in Japan were roughly half of Toyota's. The group's domestic factories were operating at half their capacity. Nissan had wound up in the red seven out of the last eight fiscal years. As a result, not counting the amount required to finance the credit Nissan offered its customers, the company's automotive debt had reached 2.1 trillion yen, more than $20 billion. Nissan continued to maintain a reputation for serious engineering, but buyers stayed away from its unexciting designs. Only one Nissan model was among the top ten best-sellers in Japan.

To understand how the company had reached this point, I spent most of spring 1999 examining Nissan from every angle: inside Japan and outside; in offices, factories, and technical centers; in conversations with suppliers, dealers, and customers. In the course of these first months, I received a new nickname: "Seven-Eleven." It was an allusion to the well-known chain of convenience stores that are as ubiquitous in Japan as they are in the United States. Like the stores, my own workdays began at dawn and ended long after sunset.

It was a period of intensive work, during which we made analyses and summaries to define the main outlines of the Nissan Revival Plan. I met people, inspected factories, and visited suppliers in Japan and in Mexico, the United States, and Europe, as well as Thailand and other countries of Southeast Asia. I asked people what they thought was going right, what they thought was going wrong, and what they would suggest to make things better. I was trying to arrive at an analysis of the situation that wouldn't be static but would identify what we could do to improve the company's performance. It was a period of intensive, active listening. I took notes, I accumulated documents that contained very precise assessments of the different situations we had to deal with, and I drew up my own personal summaries of what I learned. In the course of those three months, I must have met more than a thousand people. During that time I constructed, bit by bit, my image of the company, based on hundreds of meetings and discussions. And even though I was constantly adjusting that image, my first conclusions weren't very far from the reality of what Nissan was at the time.

The suppliers I met were very frank. They all wanted to talk to someone about their relations with Nissan, because they were deeply worried about the fix the company was in. They all had an interest in the company's recovery. And they had so much to get off their chests in regard to their relations with Nissan. I never had any problem getting them to talk, from the senior managers to the workers on the ground. In Mexico, I had meetings with suppliers in local branches that stood just outside the gates of our factory. They gave me an extremely factual description of what was going on. They drew my attention to the fragmentation of our supply system and to the fact that our forecasts were ridiculous. For a factory that built 200,000 vehicles annually, there were six tire suppliers! They didn't understand what our vision was, didn't understand our strategy or our priorities. They complained that whenever Nissan set a goal, it would be modified three months later. They gave me a very factual, very blunt description of all the malfunctions that were apparent in the company. Their meaning was clear: "You Nissan people have brought your bad performance on yourselves." The degree of frustration was so high that I never had any problem establishing a frank, open dialogue.

One of the most memorable meetings that I attended during

this exploratory phase was with Nissan's union. Like all the big Japanese enterprises, membership in the union is obligatory for all full-time employees. The new union organization had the power of de facto joint management.

The union people asked to see me in July, just after I'd been named chief operating officer and appointed to Nissan's board of directors. All Nissan's top union leaders came to the meeting. Before the meeting, Nissan's union had been described to me in very worrying terms. But I left the meeting very, very favorably impressed, because we'd all spoken very frankly. At the end, one of the union men told me, "We've had our fill of plans, especially unsuccessful ones, which is to say all those that have been presented to us until now. This company is bleeding. The employees are anxious. We have to get Nissan out of this hole. As long as we believe that you're acting constructively and taking our remarks and observations into account, we won't do anything to hinder the revival process." I was very relieved by this first meeting. The union leaders were playing their proper role. They weren't exactly obliging, but what they had to say was basically quite constructive. They left me reassured and encouraged. I knew I'd have to win their trust, but I also knew they were prepared to grant it. They were profoundly worried about their company. Their message was that if I showed I was really serious about straightening Nissan out, they wouldn't pull any unpleasant surprises. I've never taken union dealings lightly. When your employees have a union, you have to take what its members say seriously, and you have to be honest when you explain what you're doing. Considering the warnings I'd received, that meeting was like a breath of fresh air. I knew that we were going to be able to work together.

During those first months, I spent a lot more time in the lower reaches of the company than I did on the fifteenth floor of Nissan's headquarters. Despite the urgency of the situation, Nissan's legal calendar underwent no changes. At the end of June, there was to be a general assembly of Nissan's shareholders, at which Thierry Moulonguet, Patrick Pelata, and I were officially scheduled to take our seats on the company's new board of directors. Until then, we languished in a kind of legal void.

Since I didn't yet have any official function at first, I didn't attend any of Nissan's executive meetings. But Yoshikazu Hanawa had already reached an agreement with Louis Schweitzer to change the board of directors. He consulted me on the composition of the new board and the executive committee. I didn't choose any of the members of the new team because I didn't know them. I told Hanawa-*san* that I would trust him to make these decisions.

One of the first consequences of Nissan's new Alliance with Renault was the reduction of the size of the board of directors, from thirty-seven members to ten. As with many Japanese companies, the board didn't represent the shareholders but rather the company's bureaucracy. One gained a seat on the board of directors through mere length of service rather than because of any ability to conceive and carry out an effective strategy. The huge size of the board served as a screen for the ironclad supremacy of the CEO and the small circle of people around him.

Although I took no part in deciding the composition of the executive committee, I did insist on altering its structure. I wanted clear definitions of the responsibilities of the different committee members. I wanted an executive vice president in charge of purchasing, for example. Still, although the executive committee was going to become part of my team, I didn't choose its members. First of all, few of them were fluent in English, so there was the language barrier. I didn't have any way to form an opinion about them. And second, as we gradually discovered, we were dealing with a very different managerial culture. Yet when all was said and done, I wound up changing only two members of the executive committee. Two out of nine—not exactly a massacre. The other choices Yoshikazu Hanawa made were eminently suitable.

The image of Nissan that emerged from all my travels was that of a disjointed, confused company. Everyone was pulling in a different direction. We had no vision, no strategy, no priorities, no measuring tools. Everything divided up into territories, like little baronies. There was no coherence, no sense of timing. The engineers knew the products, and were technical experts, but that's not enough. No matter how competent some of its departments may be, operation of the company has to be based on a vision of the automobile business. What are our priorities? Who does what? All that was very hazy and vague. I realized that either I was going to have to shine a light everywhere, or I was going to have to have people around me whose job it was to illuminate problems so that everyone could see them clearly and know what had to be done.

How could this have occurred at one of the crown jewels of Japanese industry, a company famous for its technological expertise, a company that had shown great creativity in the past, especially in the technical innovation and design? The answer to that question wasn't some generalization about Japan's economic decline after the speculative bubble of the 1980s. Toyota and Honda, engaged in the same business in the same country, had managed to do quite well. The answer was to be found in Nissan's corporate history. But I wasn't there to do archaeological work. And obviously, I couldn't hope to learn very much on this subject from the management that had presided over the company's decline.

To tell the truth, I never met anyone in Nissan who could give me an exhaustive analysis of what had happened to it. I never went to a single place where anyone could speak about the company articulately. No one was able to offer me a summary of the problems listed in the order of their importance. Management was in complete and obvious chaos. This, I believed, was the primary cause of Nissan's difficulties. As soon as you recognize such a condition in a company, you know one thing for certain:

If its results aren't already falling, it won't be long before they'll begin to.

What did I think were the chief reasons for Nissan's plight? First, Nissan wasn't really engaged in the pursuit of profit. Managers were unaware of their own results, knew few figures, and had no precisely quantified goals. They were selling cars without knowing if they were taking losses or making profits. Few people knew this sort of thing at the senior level, and the information they got was based on scant data. Sure, executives discussed profitability, but the company wasn't managed to that end. And when profit's not a motivating element, it won't simply materialize as a result of good luck. You have to place profit at the center of your concerns. No magic is going to bring it about.

Later, a precise cost analysis we did showed some astounding results: of the forty-three different models that Nissan marketed in 1999, only four made money! The March, Nissan's entry-level vehicle, a model crucial to the company's sales volume and market share, showed a negative profit margin that exceeded 15%.

Second, there was a lot of talk about the customer at Nissan, but the customers had little presence in the company. When I wanted to know what the target clientele for such and such a product was, or why a customer would choose Nissan over one of the competition's models—questions basic to the automobile business—we got no answers. There was no product planning process that included consideration of the customer and the market. The tendency was to repeat models that already existed or to copy what the competition was doing.

Toyota was a master at this game, following its competitors like a shadow, shamelessly duplicating successful formulas, multiplying platforms and engines, bringing out a new model every month to supply five distribution networks, while ready to pull that model off the market at once if it was a flop. Nissan tried to follow Toyota and got burned.

The third factor was a lack of urgency. When we started to talk about deadlines, the Nissan people suggested time frames up to ten times longer than what I thought was reasonable. No one seemed to feel we had an emergency; no one seemed to notice that the house we were in was on fire. The notion of time didn't exist. To my shock, whenever I brought up the question of a deadline, people told me a year for what should have taken a week, and three years for something that should have been done in three months. I quickly realized I was going to have to reset the company clock.

The Japanese have a reputation for never wanting to lose face. To admit that things aren't going well is shameful. Now, it's impossible to resurrect a failing company without first diagnosing its problems and then making sure that everyone in the enterprise knows the results of your diagnosis. If there's a reticence about sharing the results, there can be no shared sense of urgency. If you don't yell, "Fire!"—if you content yourself with saying, "Hey, it's really hot in here. Maybe something's burning somewhere"— then the flames will continue to grow. You have to identify the problem and circulate your diagnosis. When we pointed out, in public, that some of Nissan's products were not all that attractive, we got a lot of criticism. People said, "You can't criticize your own products."

But it was this very statement, the frank admission that some of the products in our line weren't appealing, that allowed us to straighten things out, even if what we said may have had a short-term negative effect. There comes a time when you have to say, "I'm sick, my health is bad, and I'm embarrassed about it, but I can't get better if I don't admit it." It's not possible to ask the people around you to understand what's going on if you refuse to share the facts with them. It's painful, but it's the only way to get medicine strong enough to treat the disease. There can be debates about how to proceed, but a company's failure to look reality in the face will lead to its demise.

Fourth was the incredible compartmentalization of the company. I wasn't particularly shocked by this—I'd experienced the same phenomenon at Renault. But it was peculiarly perplexing in Nissan's case, because one of the striking things about Japanese industry is the quality of the teamwork. Although the compartmentalization of functions is a common problem in industry in general and in the automobile industry in particular, I was a little flabbergasted. I'd expected the Japanese to know how to work in cross-functional teams. Compartmentalization and territoriality aren't any more widespread in Japan than they are in France. But in France, people aren't naturally inclined to teamwork. In Japan, on the other hand, people are quite comfortable working in teams. Observing this great discrepancy between the high quality of Nissan's teamwork and the mediocrity of its cross-functional efforts was much more surprising.

This compartmentalization inside Nissan was well known to people outside the company. We had the feeling that everyone was protecting his own territory, hiding information about it from his neighbors. Such a lack of communication is extremely dangerous. When you're in a company that doesn't work cross-functionally, everyone feels satisfied with his own performance and assumes that bad results are someone else's fault. When sales and marketing post catastrophic results, the people in those departments tell themselves, "If the company provided us with attractive cars, we'd show what we can do." And the people in product planning say, "What can we do? Considering what we get from sales and marketing, it looks as though those guys just don't know how to sell cars." Everyone can tell himself that the company wouldn't be in this fix if the other departments only did a better job.

Finally—and this was one of the most important factors—the company had no strategy. If you asked people what Nissan would be in five years or ten years, or what the significance of the name Nissan was as far as they were concerned, you discovered a total absence of vision. There was a pervasive sense of the company's precariousness, a feeling of deep distress that the company was falling apart without knowing what to do to reverse the process.

CHAPTER 12

ON THE DRAWING BOARD

In a certain way, making a plan for rebuilding a company is an engineering job. It's like building a house. There are priorities, stages, limits, specifications. You begin with the foundation. You have to establish a timetable and a budget. And, of course, you have to get firm commitments on prices and deadlines.

By June 1999, I had a much clearer image of the company than I'd had in March, but it wasn't yet detailed enough to serve as a basis for taking action. Before I could go into action, I needed something much more elaborate. After I was appointed chief operating officer at the end of June, I made a determined effort to fill in the blanks. The first executive committee meeting I attended was held early in July. That was the moment when we launched the cross-functional teams.

The cross-functional teams lie at the heart of what people call my method. They were the key to the success of the Nissan Revival Plan, because they necessarily engaged those who would be charged with carrying out the plan.

I knew that if I tried to impose changes from the top down, I'd fail. That's why I decided to place a battery of cross-functional teams, or CFTs, at the center of the recovery effort. I'd used CFTs on the other occasions when I was working to turn a company around, and I'd come to the conclusion that they were an extremely powerful tool for inducing executives to look beyond the functional and spatial boundaries of their direct responsibilities. The idea was to tear down the walls, whether visible or invisible, that reduce a collective enterprise to a congregation of groups and tribes, each with their own language, their own values, their own interests. To compel people to talk to one another, to listen to one another, and to exchange knowledge. That was the essence of their power. Easier said than done, particularly when you consider that this wasn't Nissan's first revival plan. Nissan had initiated the "Global Restructuring Policy" in June 1995 and its "Plan to Reform Its Business Globally" in May 1998.

The plans that Nissan had worked up in the past were essentially qualitative. I had trouble figuring out what they were trying to do. There were no priorities, no coordination or timing. They didn't put a name or a team in front of each goal. There was no internal communication and no financial closure. It's not enough to announce, "I want to make a quality product" and let it go at that. If you don't define quality and assess its current level, if you don't state the goal you want to reach in raising that level, if you don't set timetables and deadlines and assign groups to do the work, if the plan isn't articulated, divided into sequences clear enough for people in the company to grasp—well then, nothing's going to happen. Or, in any case, not much.

I set up nine cross-functional teams that would cover the entire spectrum of the reforms I intended to make. Team number one focused on business growth—that is, new products, new services, new markets. Team number two focused on purchases, which represent 60% of a manufacturer's expenditures. Team three, manufacturing and logistics. Team four, research and development. Team five, sales and marketing. Team six, general and administrative services, which have always played a large role at Nissan. Team seven, finance. Team eight, everything that had to do with phasing out a product, a piece of equipment, or a service. Team nine, organization and value added.

At the head of each team were two leaders, members of Nissan's executive committee (with the rank of executive vice president), representing the principal functions connected to each team's assigned area of concentration. Thus, the executive vice president in charge of purchases assumed responsibility not only for his own specialty but also for research and development, in tandem with the executive vice president in charge of engineering. The finance director and his assistant led the finance teams but also those that worked on general services and organization.

Why two leaders instead of only one? I didn't want a team with an excessively limited vision of its domain. That's why we decided, for example, that Nobuo Okubo, the executive vice president in charge of research and development, and Itaru Koeda, the head of purchasing, would lead the purchasing team together.

Each team was provided with a pilot, a senior manager whose area of competence was most directly linked to the team's defined goal: a purchasing manager for the purchasing team, a manager from manufacturing for the team responsible for manufacturing and logistics, and so on.

In order to maintain a free exchange of ideas without the intimidating presence of the members of the executive committee, the pilot of each team was put in charge of the agenda and led the discussions at team meetings. It was the pilot who was the real leader of his cross-functional team.

In general, the pilots were executives with great potential who exercised responsibilities in their departments and enjoyed a high level of credibility among their subordinates. I was personally involved in the choice of the pilots, because I saw an opportunity to identify Nissan's future leaders.

Team leaders and the pilots collaborated on choosing the members of their teams. The teams were assigned one or more goals upon which they were required to concentrate their efforts. Team number one was charged with "profitable growth": opportunities for new products, brand identity, and development time required for new models, an essential parameter in the automobile industry.

The average team was made up of ten people, middle-level managers with direct responsibilities. You need ten people if you want to go fast, but even they aren't enough to go into detail in every area. For this reason, every team had subteams or cells, each with ten members as well, and these were tasked with concentrating on very specific questions. So the cross-functional team dedicated to manufacturing created four cells, which reviewed, respectively, capacity, productivity, fixed costs, and investments.

All told, some five hundred Nissan employees were mobilized for the project, which lasted from July to September. During those months, I was engaged in frequent meetings with the cross-functional teams and with management—which contributed to the elaboration of the plan and gave me the opportunity to address certain issues in one-on-one discussions so I could be sure that all the potential of the company was being mobilized. And at the same time, I was making a lot of visits in the field.

I didn't take notes from activity to activity, item A, B, C, D, E. I started with something that's very qualitative but also pretty subjective—namely, with listening to people telling me what in their opinion was going right and what was going wrong in the company, and what they thought could be done to make it better. Instead of considering the absolute value of the performance of each function, I tried to find out what were the opportunities that each function had identified for itself or that had been mentioned by other sectors.

Objective measurements were useful in some areas, such as, for example, purchases. We made an analysis of the prices Nissan paid for parts in Japan and Europe and compared them against what Renault was paying for equipment used in comparable cars. A wheel's a wheel. When it's got the same dimensions, how much does it cost in Japan and Europe when Nissan buys it, and how much when the purchaser is Renault? We asked the same thing about a brake shoe, a battery, and so on. And by making this analysis, we found that there was a 20 to 25% discrepancy for parts used in comparable cars. So this was an objective measure of poor performance.

The next step was to find out why. Was Nissan paying for higher quality or for specifications more demanding than those Renault required? No. And the prices bore no relation to brand image or performance. In fact, Nissan had too many suppliers, each of whom received volume orders that were too small to allow the economies of scale to work in their favor. Nissan's engineers were imposing specifications that didn't take into account the current industry standards and weren't necessarily a response to any specific customer demand. Engineering didn't listen to what the suppliers were saying. The company had no real vision of the business it was in.

The cross-functional teams weren't only laboratories of ideas that allowed me to mobilize the experience and the abilities of the best people in the company while breaking down structural and hierarchical barriers. The teams also tested the company's willingness to accept often radical measures that overturned established practice.

When it came to choosing the Nissan Revival Plan's goals, some of the factors were obvious. In purchases, we knew that we had a price discrepancy with Renault of between 20% and 25%. And we knew that was something we wouldn't be able to fix in six months. We pushed the team to raise its goals higher and higher, but once we achieved a reduction of 20%—after three years—I felt that we'd reached the limit. It would have been unrealistic to go farther. This wasn't a scientific conclusion. It was based on experience, on real life, and on talks with team members. There comes a time when you have to know when to stop. I'd wanted to achieve at least a 20% reduction in purchasing costs. Reaching that goal was the result of what was already a major effort, so we decided it was best to stop there.

I had suggested that a third of the savings we wanted could be achieved by modifying Nissan's engineering specifications, which were much more exacting than those of its competitors. In the beginning, the engineers didn't agree. But in working with the cross-functional teams, they were able to see for themselves that they were wrong. In fact, they themselves identified a huge number of modifications that eventually led to even more substantial savings than we had foreseen.

A special plan called "Nissan 3-3-3" concerned a further contribution from Nissan's engineering department to the plan. The reduction of production capacity—the closing of factories—was an extremely sensitive area. No carmaker anywhere in the world takes such a decision lightly. A factory can't be reduced to a row of machines. It's an interconnected group of people, a collective whole with its own history, and it's an essential element in the community where it's located. Generally speaking, a factory supports the people who live around it; entire neighborhoods, entire towns have grown up around factories. I remembered my experiences with Vilvoorde: Closing a factory amounted to major surgery. Such an action was an assault—whether in a good cause or not—on a company's physical integrity. For the Japanese, closing a factory was practically taboo. Nissan had taken such a step once before, in 1995, when, after deferring its decision as long as possible, it had finally halted the assembly line at its vast plant in Zama, west of Tokyo. This move had proved to be traumatic. Toyota had hinted for years that it was on the verge of closing an assembly plant, but it had never carried out its threat.

The utilization of manufacturing capacity in our factories was running at 50%. Bringing that up to 75% was a minimum goal. It didn't make sense to dilute our production by spreading it out over existing factories. Some sites had to be shut down. We reached the decision to close five factories because that would create the industrial structure that seemed most rational. Similarly, we decided to close 10% of our dealerships in Japan. Why not 15% or 20%? Because when we asked the cross-functional team to identify the most obvious dealerships, the dealers in the network whose territories overlapped or who fought price wars with one another, the first responses were extremely timid. After we reached a closure rate of 10%, I saw that we were starting to lose support among our own people.

It was a question of distinguishing between the possible and the impossible, of knowing how far to go without going too far. When it came to establishing goals, we took various elements into account: objective data, the cross-functional team's estimate of how far it was willing to go, the boundary between ambition and realism. If an ambitious goal seems really impossible to reach, then it destroys motivation instead of creating it. People tell one another it's a lost cause, we'll never make it. By contrast, if you set goals that are too conservative, then people think they can be reached without effort and you destroy motivation that way. We had to aim between the two. And that was a target that had to be worked out from meeting to meeting. By the end of this three-month process, we'd managed to define goals that were very rigorous but realistic at the same time.

From the beginning, I knew that an important component of the plan would be cost reduction. Another would be the sale of unessential assets. But it was absolutely necessary to offer serious encouragement to more positive efforts: rebuilding the product line, reinvesting in technology, seizing market opportunities that Nissan's enormous debt had put out of its reach. The plan was focused on a redeployment of the company and the means to achieve that redeployment. But when we presented the plan, the aspects of it that drew the most attention were the cost reductions and the asset sales. There was much less interest in the items relating to investment in the Nissan brand, the refurbishing of product planning, the renewed emphasis on technology, and the analysis of existing market opportunities. The observers knew that all this would take time—they knew that there probably wouldn't be any visible results until after the Nissan Revival Plan had concluded its term. And they felt that the thorniest part of the plan was the part that dealt with cost cutting and selling off assets, because that amounted to calling into question the company's management along with its established relationships with its partners. So at first the plan was seen as a restructuring program rather than a redeployment program. Only with the passage of time did people start to appreciate the plan in its entirety, which looked beyond short-term improvements to the redeployment of our corporate forces.

Even more than the factory closings, the dismantling of Nissan's *keiretsu* network came as a shock to Japan's business world, to the press, and to Japanese public opinion. Up until the crisis in the 1990s, the *keiretsu* system had been considered one of the foundations of the Japanese economic model, on the same level with lifetime employment in the largest corporations. The *keiretsu* weave a company into a stout web of permanent financial, human, and business relationships. In a certain sense, the company is imprisoned. But it is also protected. This organizational method was not limited to the biggest names in Japanese industry, the Mitsubishis and Sumitomos and Mitsuis. Every Japanese company stood at the center of a *keiretsu* that comprised its bank, its suppliers, its subsidiaries, and its customers. Reciprocal stock holdings, exchanges of information and personnel, and linked sales spun a veritable spider's web that held rivals and potential predators at bay. In Nissan's case, no fewer than 1,400 companies constituted its *keiretsu*, and that's counting only those in which the automaker held capital stock.

We made it clear from the beginning that we were going to dismantle Nissan's *keiretsu*. There wasn't any panic. People were reassured when we maintained our client relationships. When we sold off, we did so properly, not haphazardly. We made sure the new shareholders were people who understood the companies we put up for sale, people who would act correctly and fulfill their obligations. We didn't conduct some kind of fire sale. And the sum total of our sales was really impressive. We reached our goal, which was 500 billion yen. I had put everyone on notice that I wouldn't do anything that would adversely affect the company's recovery. Everyone knew there would be no concessions on that point. I was ready to discuss anything, but I wouldn't accept anything that would jeopardize the recovery. My cards were on the table from the beginning. People realized very quickly that some causes were lost in advance and not worth the trouble of fighting for. The fact that there was no resistance inside the company was a big help.

The future success of the plan was in large part due to the fact that it was neither imposed from the "top down," by bosses leading as though by divine right, nor did it bubble up from below in a "bottom up" process, which often results in a lowest common denominator. It resulted, in fact, from a combination of these two approaches. But above all, it was imperative to move quickly, to not get caught in the quicksand of "Japanese consensus." This idea—that no step can be taken without unanimous agreement—was, in any case, largely a myth. Japan's great industrial successions had been accomplished by individuals with very strong personalities, bosses or executives who paid little heed to conventions, often ruled like autocrats, and relished power struggles. The so-called consensus was generally nothing more than window dressing. In the automobile industry, for instance, Taiichi Ohno, the inventor of the Toyota Production System, was thought by many to have been a veritable tyrant.

If you're focusing on speed, it's not how quickly a decision is made that's important, it's how quickly the decision is carried out. You have to measure the time that elapses between the moment a problem is detected and the moment when it's effectively resolved. It's no good just measuring the time between detection and the decision to act. The Japanese are exceptionally good at execution, at carrying out decisions. But their efficiency is dependent on their belief in a goal and the means of attaining it. I've never been a supporter of the soft, passive consensus. You have a meeting, someone disagrees, and you stop there. I favor what I call the "active consensus." If someone disagrees, you stop the meeting and summon that person. The first thing to do is to make sure that there's no divergence about the goals, and this is generally the case. So then he or she must suggest an alternative method, which I measure against the hypothesis we've already advanced. We discuss the issue until one of the two recognizes the superiority of the other's approach. But we never, never question the goals. Using this system gives you two advantages: an active consensus and a guarantee of reaching the right decision. When someone disagrees, it's worth the trouble to hear the person out, even if it takes a little time, because the other person's viewpoint can lead either to your changing your position—it's happened to me—or to a better, richer final decision. The necessary element for any rapid progress is an active consensus. A passive consensus kills your speed. But a rash decision can also have difficult consequences. An active consensus allows you to optimize decision making and execution. It demands a lot of intensity and a high level of engagement. Everyone has to know that he'll get a hearing and that it's within his power to shape a decision.

This was the method we followed in carrying out the Nissan Revival Plan. The absence of resistance from within the company astonished even seasoned observers.

This lack of resistance was essentially due to the way the plan was worked out. I never said, "This is the way it's going to be!" I made sure that there was no disagreement about the goals we wanted to reach—though I have to admit that it would have been difficult for anyone to oppose a 50% debt reduction, a return to profitability, an increase in investments, and a rejuvenation of the product line. On the other hand, I welcomed any suggestions about how all this might be accomplished. The goals and the timetable for reaching them weren't negotiable, but in compensation the question of execution was the subject of wide-open debate. We asked everyone who had good ideas to share them with us. Before we made a decision, anything was possible, but ideas had to be supported by strong arguments. Because we were aiming for results, our goals went beyond good intentions. And once the decision was taken, the discussion was over. There could be some eventual adjustments, but no substantial changes. This approach encouraged a lot of people to speak their minds. When some of them opposed the plant closings, I asked them what else we could do. I told them I wouldn't do it if someone came up with a better solution. Frank discussions about solutions clarified everyone's thinking. After the announcement, people assured one another that there had really been no other choice.

In certain areas, the debates were vigorous. There were some suppliers whom Nissan's engineers regarded as part of the company's strategic assets—not mere suppliers, but storehouses of the expertise and technological knowledge essential to Nissan's future. This was the case with JATCO, a transmission manufacturer. Nissan was at once its biggest customer and principal shareholder. JATCO had developed a real marvel, the CVT, the automatic gearbox of the future.

We had some interesting sessions where some people defended Nissan's interests in JATCO and other companies. I was willing to maintain our participation in JATCO, but only under certain conditions: It had to put together a restructuring plan, get back on the path to growth, and open itself to other manufacturers. If those things weren't done, we'd sell it. I was quite flexible about how to accomplish the goals, but I wouldn't compromise on the goals themselves. JATCO had to return to profitability, reduce its debt, and increase its market share. As for methods, I said, "Here's my plan. If you give me a better one, I'll take it." Determination and inflexibility are two different things.

The upshot of all this was that Nissan didn't sell JATCO, although it was thoroughly restructured. In 2001, it entered into a partnership with Mitsubishi Motors' own transmission business, thus becoming part of one of the biggest automatic transmission manufacturers in the world.

The area where there was most resistance to the plan was the part that called for the reorganization of Nissan's domestic commercial network. We've made some major changes, but to this day I consider that to be one of the company's weak points. Back then, it was plagued by incompetence and bureaucracy, weighed down by traditional connections, and weakened by a lack of transparency. There was also a lack of strategy. It was one of our real disaster areas.

It was also an area where changes would require the most time to take effect.

Throughout the summer of 1999, the cross-functional teams studied their assigned areas and, one after another, their proposals made their way to Nissan's executive committee for validation.

. . .

By late September, I had a much clearer idea of the company's strengths, its weaknesses, and its potential. I was ready to make my decisions. In fact, all the decisions that defined the Nissan Revival Plan were taken in the course of a relatively short period of time, perhaps a week, at the end of that three-month period. My decisions were made at the end of September, and that gave us two weeks to put the package into shape, clear the lines of communication, and prepare the company for the deployment of the new goals before I announced them on October 18, 1999. That was the day when we unveiled the NRP, stating that it would go into effect on April 1, 2000. We planned to spend the intervening time, about five and a half months, elaborating and deploying the plan, knowing that the stopwatch was set to start on the first of April.

These days, people wonder why so many Japanese corporate leaders freeze when circumstances require them to act. I don't think it's because they don't want to take action. It's because they don't know how. It's as simple as that. They lack a strategic vision. I don't mean some hazy theory but a set of clear, simple ideas accompanied by priorities that people have to agree on. Then there's the question of how to transform strategy into a plan of action and what contribution that plan requires from each of the thousands of people the company employs. All that requires a level of expertise. It's not something you can make up on the spot. When I announced my diagnosis, many people in the company were shocked. That meant that they had no real grasp of the situation. So when I declared that we were going to reduce the number of our suppliers, they found themselves in a different world, one they'd never even vaguely imagined. We went into great detail about the perspectives to be considered and the measures to be taken. If I might make a comparison, Nissan's traditional management was a little like an Indian witch doctor who uses a home-brewed concoction of plants to cure dysentery and then one day finds himself face-to-face with a modern physician armed with medications, antibiotics, and the scientific method. We arrived with a complete toolbox, but we were working with people who didn't know how to use the tools it contained. This had nothing to do with any resistance to change. The best proof of that is the fact that as soon as we started using our tools, everything clicked. And I suspect that's a situation you can find in many companies that are currently in trouble. Some people just don't know how to do what must be done. Since they don't want to lose face, they dig in their heels. As a result, they're immobile. It's a question of competence and know-how, but also of engagement. Of course, all these things are connected. It's hard to be engaged without a modicum of self-confidence and without being conscious of what it is you're looking for.

I wouldn't say we were questioning Nissan's executive recruitment, because I think there are people at Nissan who are brilliant, very intelligent. If Nissan had one recognized competitive advantage, it came from its being based in Tokyo, where it could attract the best minds in the graduating classes of the best universities in the country. The problem was what to do with them after they joined the company. Even the best recruits, the ones with the highest potential, will accomplish nothing without some direction. You have to solicit their collaboration, you have to demand a lot from them, and you have to give them challenging goals. If not, they'll gradually waste away. One may have a beautiful physique, but if it's not put to work, it atrophies. We had many talented people who'd never been asked to collaborate on really important company projects. When they took initiatives, no one was interested. Lots of people told me, "We pointed out this problem five years ago, but we didn't get any response from management, and our ideas never became part of any plan." When a company is without a powerful, shared strategy, then it becomes uncoordinated, it loses its soul, and its people are left on their own.

Our awareness of symptoms doesn't mean much. It's more important to agree on a diagnosis of the problem, and even more important to set up a plan that corresponds to the analysis. And then, once you've accomplished all that, you still haven't done more than about 5% of the work. The remaining 95% lies ahead of you; now it's a matter of execution. If you take a look at some of Nissan's previous plans, you'll see that they stopped at those initial percentages. And compared with the enormity of the problems that the company had to face, those few tentative steps meant nothing. And that's why they never produced any results. The management was trying to cure a serious illness by administering little shots in the arm.

CHAPTER 13

SHOCK THERAPY

On October 18, 1999, we invited the many journalists from
around the world who had gathered in Tokyo to cover the
Tokyo Motor Show to a rather unusual preview presentation.
These members of the international press represented publications specializing in the automotive industry as well as general
news organizations. But there were no hostesses to greet them, no
champagne, no petits fours, and, up on the stage, no gleaming
"concept car." They were presented instead with hard figures, a
severe diagnosis, and some demanding commitments.

My presentation of the Nissan Revival Plan inaugurated a
style of communication previously unknown in Japan. It took
place in the reception hall of a large hotel; huge screens were set
up, and a sequence of slides passed across those screens, complete
with numbers, curves, graphs, and texts in Japanese and English.
At the appointed time, Yoshikazu Hanawa, Nissan's president and
CEO, dressed in a dark suit and wearing a sober tie, made his
entrance. Hanawa conveyed to the audience the determination
that characterized our new management. Then Hanawa introduced me, declaring that it was "a day of unprecedented importance for Nissan's future."

My analysis of the company had given me three key numbers,
which I quickly shared with the audience.

"Since 1991, Nissan's share in the global market has been in
continuous decline. We've dropped from a 6.6% share in the world

market in 1991 to a 4.9% share today. During this period of time, our annual production has fallen by 600,000 vehicles." This drop in production was roughly equal in volume to the total annual output of an automaker of the size, say, of Volvo or Mercedes.

"Nissan has had difficulty maintaining profitability since 1991. In six of the last seven years, including our forecasts for 1999, we've lost money." In fact, fiscal year 1999, which ended on March 31, 2000, would show a record loss for Nissan—684 billion yen, more than $6 billion—accentuated by the heavy scouring the company's books had received by our new management team. We had to settle with the past to prepare the future.

"Nissan has been and remains a heavily indebted company. Our net automotive debt, without counting the sales financing we provide to our customers, amounted to over 2,100 billion yen at the end of fiscal year 1998. At the rate of 110 yen per dollar, that comes to approximately $19.4 billion." Even after the injection of capital by Renault in the spring of 1999, Nissan's debt burden remained formidable: 1,400 billion yen, about $12.6 billion, more than twice the company's equity capital.

I summarized in a few phrases my diagnosis of Nissan's problems: the failure to concentrate on profit making; the company's neglect of its customers; its weakness in cross-functional work; the general absence of a sense of urgency; the lack of a common, long-term vision. But I also reminded the audience of Nissan's accomplishments:

"Nissan has established a significant international presence and is deployed on a global scale; Nissan has developed a world-class production system; in several crucial areas, Nissan is on the cutting edge of technology; and Nissan has formed an alliance with Renault."

After explaining the method we used to devise the Nissan Revival Plan and the work of the cross-functional teams, I announced Nissan's projects for new-product development. I summed up my approach in a single sentence:

"As you know, in the automobile business, there's no problem at a car company that good products can't solve."

I reviewed Nissan's brand image, which I described as so poor that the company was forced to sell comparable products at lower prices than its competitors; its design division, "which has not always been an asset"; and the pace of its new-product development, a time frame that I intended to reduce significantly. I then discussed the opportunities opened up by Nissan's Alliance with Renault, principally European distribution and a presence in South America.

"Our goal is to reduce our purchasing costs by 20% in the course of the next three years. We have too many suppliers. According-ing to our estimates, we work with 1,145 firms that provide parts and materials. There will be no more than 600 of those by 2002. In equipment and services, we have 6,900 suppliers. By 2002, that number will be no more than 3,400." Purchases account for more than 60% of a carmaker's expenditures. I planned to eliminate the practice of negotiating these costs locally or regionally; deals would now be made on a global basis. The "Nissan 3-3-3" program called for the company's engineering and purchasing divisions to collab-orate with its suppliers to systematize cost reductions, revise speci-fications, and put the "best practices" into general use.

"Our suppliers play a vital role in our success," I told the audi-ence. "We will help those who are going to help us."

Next, I turned to Nissan's factories, which, I observed, were among the best in the world:

"When I was with Renault, Nissan's factory in Sunderland, England, was my standard of reference. And Nissan's plant in Smyrna, Tennessee, is one of the top factories in North America." The problem was that Nissan had too many factories, especially in Japan. We had enough capacity to build 2,400,000 vehicles annually. But in 1999, we produced only 1,280,000. We were using only 53% of our capacity. That overcapacity was devouring capital.

"We have decided to reduce our current capacity by 30%, which will bring it down to 1,650,000 vehicles," I told the audience. "If we cautiously predict that our production in Japan will have risen by 5.5% in 2002, that will mean a total of 1.35 million vehicles, equivalent to an 82% rate of capacity utilization. Therefore, we are going to effect the closing of the following factories: In the category of assembly plants, Murayama, Nissan Shatai in Kyoto, and Aichi Kikai in Minato in March 2001; and the Kurihama and Kyushu powertrain plants will be closed in March 2002."

My goal was to have fewer and simpler factories. In 1999, Nissan Japan had twenty-four manufacturing platforms in seven factories; by 2004, there would be no more than four vehicle assembly plants, utilizing a total of twelve car platforms. We reduced the number of powertrain combinations by a third.

But headquarters would also feel the pinch. "Our goal is to reduce by 20% our general expenses, including marketing and administrative expenses, which are very high compared to those of the best companies in the automotive industry."

Next I addressed our sales network in Japan:

"In order to instill a stronger feeling of company spirit into our distribution network, we intend to reduce the number of our subsidiaries by 20%. In addition, we will close 10% of our dealerships, thus reducing territorial overlaps and competition among Nissan dealers."

Then I was ready to tackle Nissan's *keiretsu*:

"Today, Nissan owns stock in 1,394 companies; in more than half of these, Nissan's holdings exceed 20%. With the exception of our participation in four companies, none of these holdings is considered indispensable to Nissan's future." The days of our historical, sentimental, and personal bonds between Nissan and its affiliates were over. "This means that we're going to divest ourselves of most of our holdings, and our decisions will be based strictly on a cost/benefit analysis. Our goal is to free up capital currently invested in nonstrategic assets and apply it to the core of our business, while at the same time significantly reducing our general indebtedness."

I had been outraged to discover that Nissan's ownership share in its Japanese competitor, Fuji Heavy Industries, manufacturers of Subaru vehicles, was roughly equivalent to the capital resources that would have allowed Nissan, years ago, to make improvements in its entry-level vehicle, the Nissan March. Although this model represented a critical percentage of the company's market share, the funds necessary to keep it up-to-date had been tied up in one of Nissan's competitors. As a result, the March had remained unchanged for more than a decade.

Finally, I discussed the social price that we would have to pay for Nissan's past management's mistakes. Nissan had more than 148,000 employees worldwide.

"Our forecast for fiscal year 2002 calls for 127,000 full-time employees. This will mean the elimination of 21,000 jobs, about 14% of Nissan's total workforce," I told those gathered.

The ax fell evenly on manufacturing (we eliminated 4,000 jobs), our sales network in Japan (resulting in 6,500 layoffs), and general and administrative services (6,000 jobs). The only exception was the company's research-and-development division, which was slated to add 500 positions.

The numbers were harsh, I told the audience, but I promised my methods would be gentle:

"The reduction of the workforce will be accomplished through natural departures, an increase in part-time work, sales of subsidiaries, and early retirements. We're going to proceed very smoothly, particularly in the manufacturing division in Japan."

As a counterpart to this intense, unprecedented effort, I made three commitments. They would be the standard against which the success or failure of the Nissan Revival Plan would be measured.

First, a return to profitability in fiscal year 2000.

Second, a profit margin in excess of 4.5% of sales by fiscal year 2002.

And third, a 50% reduction in the current level of debt.

"I know and I measure how much effort, how much sacrifice, and how much pain we will have to endure for the success of the Nissan Revival Plan. But believe me, we don't have a choice, and it will be worth it. We all shared a dream: a dream of a reconstructed and revived company, a dream of a thoughtful and bold Nissan on track to perform profitable growth in a balanced alliance with Renault to create a major global player in the world car industry. This dream becomes today a vision with the Nissan Revival Plan. This vision will become a reality as long as every single Nissan employee will share it with us."

. . .

The shock of my announcement was part of Nissan's therapy. My task had been to make public opinion, both outside and (especially) within the company, understand and admit that Nissan had reached the point of no return. Consequently, the "surprise" factor was an essential element of the announcement. And the publication of the plan had the effect of a sort of earthquake.

Throughout the negotiations that resulted in the Renault-Nissan Alliance, Renault executives were surprised to find the proposed alliance the subject of a steady stream of information and rumors published in the business sections of the Japanese daily newspapers. Although confidentiality was a requisite in dealings of this type, it seemed to be systematically breached by sources inside Nissan at the very highest levels. This state of affairs had to do, in large part, with the nature of the traditional relationships between the press and other institutions in Japan.

The reason there weren't any leaks about the contents of the plan before my presentation was that it stayed in the executive committee until the day I announced it. Even the Japanese government was only apprised of it right before the presentation. I wanted at all costs to avoid leaks. Why was I so adamant about leaks? Because the plan couldn't be understood unless it was considered in its entirety. If news of the plan had come out bit by bit—"They're going to close three plants; they're going to cut the number of suppliers in half; they're going to sell their stock"—it would have been a disaster. It would have resulted only in frightening people. It was absolutely necessary to present the complete plan all at once.

The post-presentation press conference gave a foretaste of what was to come the next day, October 19, when headlines around the world showed that I had achieved the effect I'd sought.

The foreign media gave the plan a lot of attention because it was the first time that a program of that scope, with such precise detail and such a level of commitment, had been put in place in Japan. There was applause in the hall at the end of the presentation on October 18. I was surprised, because nobody ever applauds at a press conference. I'm sure people were applauding because they were glad that someone had had the courage to break a whole series of taboos that Japanese companies had been suffering from for years. I felt right away that the American press in particular wanted the plan to succeed. The Americans probably figured it would serve as a kind of wake-up call for all Japan. Those journalists were delighted to see something like that happen in a model company like Nissan.

But the crucial battle for the success of the plan was the battle for public opinion inside the company. Nissan's employees were the people most conscious of our problems. At the same time, they were the ones who had been disappointed most often by Nissan management's unkept promises. In order to get everyone's attention, I made a very specific commitment during the press conference following my presentation: If any one of the stated goals in three major areas—return to profitabililty, debt reduction, and operating profit margin—were not met within the time frame and at the stipulated level, I would resign, and with me would resign all the other members of Nissan's executive committee.

That is what made the deepest impression on people inside the company—the fact that I made a commitment to profitability, in my own name and in the name of all the other executive committee members. There was obviously no way that I could be held responsible for the current state of the company or for what had happened to it before the Alliance. Nevertheless, I was putting my job and my future on the line if I failed to deliver on any one of the three commitments outlined in the plan. People were really struck by that. They saw our determination, and they knew that we could never back down from such a public commitment. If Nissan hadn't made a clear return to profitability by the end of fiscal year 2000, I was going to resign, as were all the other members of the executive committee, and someone else would take charge of Nissan's future. This declaration caused a certain amount of turmoil. Our people were quite struck—they realized that we were serious. They saw that watering down the plan or delaying its application or striving for only 80% of the stipulated goals was out of the question. There was no debate. We had to achieve everything we'd committed ourselves to.

Another important factor was that the plan, in comparison to all previous Japanese corporate plans, was very precise, extremely factual, and highly quantified, not only in relation to the performance we meant to achieve but also in relation to the deadlines we set. The plan left little room for interpretation. The message couldn't be softened. When you announce that you're going to close five plants and you give a timetable for the closings, and when you say there's going to be a 20% reduction in purchasing costs and 33% of that is going to come from collaboration with the engineering division, when everything is quantified, then there's no choice; if you disagree with the plan, you've got to leave the company.

. . .

The plan was simultaneously announced to Nissan's 148,000 employees: in offices, in factories, in research centers, and in dealerships at the same time as my presentation.

In fact, I told the audience that the other members of the executive committee were absent because they were getting ready to pass on my message and give out information about the plan to everyone in the company.

Before the announcement of the plan, the anxiety was pervasive. When I visited the factories during the summer, I saw anxiety everywhere. Everyone could see that the shops weren't working to full capacity. It was obvious that we had a lot of unused capacity, a lot of underutilized skilled employees. Everyone knew that something was going to happen. People were worried, hoping they themselves wouldn't be affected by whatever measures we decided on. When I announced the plant closings, the bad atmosphere that had pervaded the company disappeared. Some people's worst fears were realized, but others were relieved, and doubts were replaced by certainties. At least the unfortunate workers whose plants were to be shut down knew exactly when that would happen. And the others were reassured about their future roles in Nissan's production.

The Japanese authorities didn't exactly applaud the announcement of the NRP. On the other hand, the administration didn't interfere with us in any way. The Japanese government took a decidedly neutral position. One of the reasons they did so was that they realized this was a serious effort to get Nissan out of the hole it was in. They were quite worried about the impact that a Nissan collapse would have on the Japanese economy, on local communities, on suppliers, and on automobile dealers.

A lot of time had to pass before we could be confident that the plan was correctly deployed throughout the company. Because the execution of the plan didn't effectively begin until April 1,

2000, we took many steps to get ready for the launch. We chose a date nearly six months away so that we'd have time to deploy the plan and make sure that everyone in the company understood their individual responsibilities and knew the nature of the contribution they were expected to make. As for me, I basically concentrated on Japan, because this was the country involved in the most difficult part of the plan. In the United States, we eliminated some jobs in administrative services, marketing, and sales and we closed our offices in New York and Washington, but, all things considered, these steps were far from drastic. The most severe measures affected Japan.

Initially, we endured a lot of criticism, especially from a few suppliers, but also from the press and some industry analysts, who thought—with some justification—that an automobile manufacturer shouldn't alienate such essential partners. There were two chief questions: Are they really going to do what they said they were going to do in the time frame they stipulated? And aren't they going to demoralize the company, alienate their suppliers, and develop quality problems? The decision to reduce from five to three the number of Japanese steel producers working for Nissan was publicly challenged. "Toyota would never act in such a way," declared Yoichi Shimogaichi, CEO of NKK Steel, which Nissan was retaining as one of its suppliers, but after reducing its business together by half. But there was never any notion of playing Nissan off against its suppliers. We were trying to construct a system that would increase Nissan's chances of survival. We told them, "We understand that some of you won't be able to follow us, but we'll have long-term relationships with the ones who do. We'll remember that you stood by us when times were hard, that you were willing to roll up your sleeves and take part in the NRP."

The Nissan Revival Plan represented a revolution of sorts for the Japanese economy. Not for its social effects, which were as moderate as implementation of the plan would allow, but for its effects on standards and practices that had been in place for decades and were associated, rightly or wrongly, with the success of the Japanese economic model. Of all the broken taboos—some would say, of all the sacred myths destroyed—the most significant, without a doubt, was the Japanese notion that there should be no winners and no losers. Advancement by seniority, unlimited public support for noncompetitive sectors and companies, the appearance of egalitarianism in social relations—all these were based on the idea that Japan's performance was a collective enterprise and that no one should be abandoned on the side of the road. We made a clean break with the Japanese idea that no one should win and no one should lose, the idea that a company was obligated to protect all its employees. What caused the break was the fact that Nissan was about to go down and drag all its suppliers down with it. The damage done would have been infinitely greater if there had been no plan or if the plan hadn't succeeded. The whole corporation was headed for catastrophe, and the number of jobs at risk would have been ten times greater, both inside and outside the company. You can't say that there was a choice between maintaining the status quo and executing the NRP. That's not true. That's deceiving people. The status quo was not possible for Nissan. The company was at an impasse. We had reached the end of our rope. The company, despite its size, its name, and its history, had been evaluated and dismissed as lost by two world-class automotive manufacturers, DaimlerChrysler and Ford. Jac Nasser, Ford's CEO, said, "We don't want to waste our hard-earned money paying off careless debts." These were two serious competitors, and at a time they were feeling particularly hungry—Ford was in the process of buying Volvo, and Daimler had just taken on Chrysler and was moving into Mitsubishi. But they weighed Nissan and found it wanting. They couldn't assume the risk of taking on such an operation.

Nissan was facing success or failure, period. As time would tell, Renault turned out to be the ideal partner. We played the right card, and we had a good plan that produced positive results. Today, the fact that Nissan is rehiring, reinvesting, and granting wage increases shows that the process we instituted wasn't destructive; it was creative. But an essential step in creation is facing reality.

CHAPTER 14

YOU HAVE TO
COM-MU-NI-CATE

When I joined Nissan, the company had to contend with a total lack of credibility: lack of credibility in the brand, lack of credibility in the company, and—let's face it—lack of credibility in the Alliance. I think it was Ferdinand Piech, the former head of Volkswagen, who said that two mules can't make a racehorse.

Credibility rests on two pillars. First of all, performance: If you don't perform, you're not credible. And second, transparency. Even when you're not performing well, transparency can help you. Well, as far as performance was concerned, we didn't have anything. We were a tabula rasa, a blank page. There wasn't much that we could count on in that area. The only choice remaining was to play the transparency card. I remembered the Perrier affair over tainted water. They recognized that they had a problem right away; they said, "We have a problem, and we're dealing with it." If you've made a mistake, say so and start fixing it!

Within forty-eight hours, the firm had identified the source of the traces of benzene in some of its batches of water, made all information available to the public, and ordered the recall of all the batches of Perrier that were then in circulation. It was an expensive operation, but it saved the company from a much more serious disaster, the loss of its customers' confidence. Ever since then, Perrier has been a textbook study in crisis handling and communication.

Because I was convinced of the value of transparency, I insisted from the very beginning that Nissan's transparency would be total. We were going to speak openly about our problems and our results. If our results were good, we'd say so, but if they were poor, we'd say that, too. And the NRP was comparatively transparent. We said what we were doing wrong and we named the problems we were going to address. We had to reestablish our credibility at all costs. We had to communicate.

From the first weeks following the formation of the Alliance, I had initiated a series of meetings with the press. I held informal briefing sessions for small groups, with the Tokyo correspondents of the international press on one side and local journalists on the other. Jackets were removed, and the dialogue—in English—was open and generally "on the record." For the CEO of a great Japanese corporation, this sort of thing was utterly extraordinary. The *koho*, Nissan's communications department, had trouble keeping up with me. For a while, it opposed my giving live interviews on TV Asahi's 10 o'clock evening news program—hosted by Hiroshi Kume, the least conventional and most popular news announcer in Japan—on the grounds that it was necessary to give priority to the more respectable public network, NHK. I opened the doors of my professional and even my personal life to international magazines such as *Business Week* and *Paris Match*, as well as numerous Japanese publications. Readers learned about my typical day, about my factory visits, about my dinners with my family. Some people thought that I was, in fact, going too far in this direction, but it was a move I had thought about carefully.

In crisis, communication has to be concentrated. You can't have fifteen people talking at the same time, because they're not all going to say the same thing in the same way. It was obvious from the start that the head of the company had to be the one doing the communicating and that I had to communicate a lot of information about the plans I'd made and how I was carrying them out. It's my responsibility to do that. This was a choice made to reestablish the company's credibility. Some people talk about a personality cult or megalomania. Well, I've been in professional life since 1978, and when I was with Michelin, I wasn't on the front pages of the newspapers. That really wasn't the company's style. When I was with Renault, I was a bit more visible, but that was because I had an unusual background, not because of any desire on my part to be in the spotlight. With Nissan, I was more visible out of necessity.

Obviously, communication isn't limited to features in the style of *People* magazine. Every six months, Nissan publishes its semi-annual and annual results. We try to make our "show" a model of transparency. The presentation is given in Japanese and English, graphs are projected onto a giant screen for everyone in the room to see, and I conduct the presentation.

In recent years, Japan has gradually moved into conformity with Western-style norms of corporate governance. Nissan was among the very first companies listed on the Tokyo Stock Exchange to present consolidated accounts, overturning the traditional practice of Japanese corporations, which had been to publish the accounts of the parent company only, thereby covering up the losses on the balance sheets of its subsidiaries. So in October 2000, on the one-year anniversary of the announcement of the Nissan Revival Plan, I called a press conference to deliver a progress report. I gave the media both the good news—Nissan's financial recovery had occurred earlier than expected—and the bad news—the continuing decline of the company's market share in Japan. As a result, the front-page headlines of October 1999—"Nissan's in bad shape"—were replaced by "Nissan's coming back" in October 2000. The balance sheet for the first half (April–September) of fiscal year 2000 showed a spectacular reversal of the trends that had produced record losses the previous year. But there was still a great deal of skepticism about Nissan outside the company, despite all the evidence of change.

At this stage, personal information about me was being communicated to the public much more successfully than the message of Nissan's revival. I was told that the Japanese frequently go through periods of infatuation with people who are in the public eye. They seemed to succumb to "Ghosn-mania." I frequently appeared on magazine covers and became a role model in a country anxious for strong leadership. I was offered as an example to politicians to help lift the country out of its economic doldrums.

My kids laughed at the whole thing. They'd say, "Look, Daddy's on TV again," or "We saw your picture in the subway." When my book *Renaissance* was published in Japan, they asked for a life-size advertising poster with a picture of me to show to their friends. Two days later, it was in the trash.

But the media situation presented Nissan with some obvious problems and opportunities. How could we gradually transfer this capital to the Nissan brand itself?

There were two sorts of articles—those about me, and those about Nissan. On the one hand, you've got me as an individual: my personality, my history, the interviews, the fact that I've got an original way of looking at things. But no matter how different or original you may be, if you don't produce results, you're just a clown. On the other hand, I'm not unpopular inside the company. We talk about things that resonate with other people. To my good fortune, I came to Japan at a time when the country was going through a period of self-examination. If Japan had never started asking itself questions, I would have had to go about things differently. It wouldn't have been an impossible mission, just a different one. You have to adapt your strategy to fit your circumstances.

Earlier, in June 2000, Nissan's new management had to submit its accounts to the annual meeting of the company's shareholders for the first time. Taking advantage of the lack of transparency in the management of Japanese companies, I was told that professional extortionists known as *sokaiya* often try to exact payment in return for suppressing questions from stockholders. If a company fails to yield to their demands, the *sokaiya* throws the meeting into turmoil with embarrassing revelations. (Lately, strict laws have changed this.)

Before the first annual shareholders' meeting I attended, I was warned that there could be disturbances, that people might be there to ask provocative or unfair questions. I was told, "They're looking for a reaction. The questions they ask and the attitudes they display will never make page one, but if you react even a bit too strongly, you'll be in all the headlines."

An individual started the proceedings by criticizing those of us who were French for not having bowed deeply enough before taking our seats on the platform. He monopolized the meeting for more than an hour. Yoshikazu Hanawa, who was chairing the session, was unable to interrupt him. Standing at the podium, I was growing impatient.

That was my premiere. The next year, we introduced some changes. Yoshikazu Hanawa took care of the introduction and the conclusion; I handled the rest, and I took questions after the presentation. Questions are never a problem. What counts is the way you answer them. In 2001, there were a lot of provocative questions, but by then we understood the system and tried to give the most constructive answers possible, even to those who would attempt to disrupt the meeting. But we also imposed a time limit on questioners, because we received complaints from shareholders who hadn't had the chance to have their say. When I cut off one of the questioners, things started to get a little warm in the room. But then the individual asking the questions calmed down and we went on to other things. Of course, our financial results were a lot better that year, and that made our job easier.

My essential task from the beginning was to establish lines of communication with our shareholders in order to persuade them, too, to renew their faith in the company.

We make a deliberate effort to improve communications,

especially when it comes to keeping our Japanese shareholders informed. This can be done in different ways. First of all, through transparency: We talk to Japanese and foreign analysts and explain to them what we're doing. Of course, good numbers provide the most convincing demonstrations of our success. And in this respect, the rising value of Nissan's stock has been the clearest indicator of public opinion.

When the Alliance agreement was signed, shares of Nissan stock were going for around 400 yen. Then the price rose to between 550 and 580 yen, but it fell again after we announced the Nissan Revival Plan. Why? Not because analysts were opposed to the plan but because they didn't think we'd reach our goals by the deadlines we set. And since I had announced that we'd all resign if our commitments weren't kept, people thought that maybe this wasn't the right moment to back Nissan. Besides, we had also said that we were going to divest ourselves of our reciprocal stocks— that is, we were going to sell our stock in other companies— and this led analysts to believe that those companies would in turn dump their Nissan stock and so lower its market value. On April 1, 2000, our stock was at 410 yen. By mid-2004, our share price hovered near 1,200 yen in a market that had fallen by around 45% over the same period of time. Performance trumps everything. That's what gives a company its life.

Over the decades-long period of its decline, people had lost faith in Nissan, both as a brand and as a company. To rebuild that faith and make it last, it was essential that Nissan execute its new, transparent policy of continually making public its commitments and goals. This was true for its "public" inside and outside the company. Employees are citizens, too, people who read newspapers and watch television. In other words, reconstructing our public image involved convincing our employees as well as our stockholders of our mission.

Everything I've been able to do has been based on motivating our people. All our accomplishments start from there. At a low point in October 1999, the question was How can we make the most of Nissan's human capital, how can we motivate our people? That was the only way to start climbing out of the hole we were in. Motivating our employees was an essential step in the company's recovery. And one of our top priorities was to assess what we could do to reinforce that motivation. We offered financial incentives, we conferred awards, we gave promotions, we negotiated with the unions. But the most significant thing we did was to present a completely different vision of the company. We said: If we reach our goals, this is what we'll be in two years and this is what we'll be in five years.

Generally speaking, only the public can determine the perception, the image of a company. The company can set benchmarks and indicate what it wishes to become. It offers a model, an ideal. I may know I'll never reach that ideal, but I also know that I must always strive for it. It's your own vision of what the company ought to be. People see the company from the outside, the same way they look at you. They don't know what your vision is. They look at your products, they assess your personality, and they say, "That's Nissan," or "That's Honda." To rebuild a brand image and a company image, you have to do several things. First, you have to define an ideal; you have to orient the company in such a way that every decision made tends toward that ideal. Once you've done that, the public—customers and others—observes the company, looks at its ads, listens to its messages, uses its services, meets its representatives, and perhaps buys its products. In the process, people form an image of your ideal, as they perceive it, and they reflect that back to you. That's why it's absurd to declare, "We're Nissan, and this is what we are." The most you can say is "This is what we want to be." And that's exactly what's happening today. We've never said that we wanted to be perceived as this or that. We work on creating an image. But it's up to the public to decide what that image is, and it's up to us to observe the evolution of our brand image in the eyes of the general public.

That evolution has reflected the stages of Nissan's rebirth: financial recovery; the launch of new models more and more representative of the make's new image; a return to investments and hiring; and the stabilization, followed by the rise, of the company's market share. And all of this has been underlined by strikingly effective public relations and advertising campaigns. Were we successful? In January 2004, in the *Financial Times* "World's Most Respected Companies" ranking list for 2003, Nissan was 34th. The *Financial Times* also compiles annual lists of the world's 50 most respected business leaders, based on interviews with 1,000 senior executives and opinion makers in 20 countries. I was fortunate enough to be listed 4th. In May 2004, when the *Financial Times* released its Global Top 500 ranking of the largest companies by market capitalization, Nissan was 84th. In June 2004, *Newsweek* published a ranking of the Global Top 500 corporations. Nissan, at 68th, was the top carmaker. (The rankings were based on turnover, return on equity, financial standings, and corporate social responsibility.) The other carmakers featured in the list were BMW (71st), Honda (79th) and Toyota (87th).

CHAPTER 15

DESIGN, DEVELOP,
FINANCE, SELL

I understood from the beginning that the success of the Alliance would depend heavily on Renault's and Nissan's ability to preserve and reinforce their respective brand identities. And in the automobile industry, perhaps more than in any other industry, the brand image is a function of product design. Nissan's design could not be perceived as a carbon copy of Renault's. This was all the more essential in that Renault's design, under the leadership of its design director, Patrick Le Quément, had an exceptionally strong sense of personality. All you had to do was to step into some of Nissan's showrooms or try to identify its models on the street to understand that this was an aspect of the company that required nothing less than a revolution.

We realized from the moment we arrived that our design department needed some new blood. Nissan had two problems in this area. First of all, design was subordinated to the director of engineering. This was an absurd situation, an umbilical cord that needed to be cut. We cut design loose from engineering and put it under the leadership of Patrick Pelata, the head of product planning. We could have just gone out and hired the most talented and creative people we could find, but if we'd left them under the control of the technicians, I'm not sure we would have seen so much imagination and daring from our design team. Second, we had to find a design head who could symbolize Nissan's revival, someone who had worked outside the company, someone with sufficient self-confidence and an international vision. He would have to be capable of reinstilling confidence in the design teams, and he had to be someone who hadn't been affected by Nissan's past, when design was dependent on engineering. We discussed what we wanted with Patrick Le Quément, and he assisted in the search using a headhunter based in the United States. I let Pelata, Le Quément, and a few other collaborators make the preselection. It came down to two choices, both Japanese designers. I interviewed them both and opted for Shiro Nakamura.

Shiro Nakamura, who wore thin, round eyeglasses, a trim mustache, dressed invariably in black, seemingly the preferred color of designers. Nakamura worked for Isuzu Motors, a Japanese carmaker that General Motors had taken under its wing. Isuzu specializes in all-terrain vehicles. Shiro Nakamura had made a name for himself with a virile, muscular style, a style that provoked strong reactions. To Nissan's four hundred designers, the arrival of an "outsider," a veteran of such a relatively small manufacturer as Isuzu, came as a shock if not a humiliation.

Maybe the other designers would have accepted an American or a Frenchman more readily, but such a head of design would inevitably have been criticized for not understanding Japan and not being able to communicate. For the position I had in mind, I felt a Japanese outsider was the best choice. I think that's true for other key functions at Nissan as well, including my own. The best person to lead the company through the changes that I've instituted would have been a Japanese outsider with strong industrial experience, an open mind, and a history of working in other countries. But when the right Japanese outsider can't be found, the next-best choice is a foreigner from outside.

People ask me if being a foreigner is an advantage to me. Not at all, I would say. Being Japanese would have been an asset as a

CEO—but a Japanese leader with a global vision and a good deal of experience in the industry. I felt the most important factor was that the person be someone from outside the company, given Nissan's situation. We needed someone who didn't carry all the baggage of the company's history; he had to have a degree of credibility that would have been difficult for someone from the inside to achieve.

. . .

From the moment I arrived in Japan, one of my first instincts was to bring back the "Z." The Datsun 240Z wasn't a car, it was a legend. Called by some "the poor man's Jaguar XKE," this inexpensive sport coupe had been a triumphant success, particularly in the United States. Datsun sold more than a million Zs, a world record for a sports car. But the Z—now the Nissan 300ZX—had not aged gracefully: It had become too heavy, too expensive, too sophisticated. In 1996, Nissan, short on cash, decided to bring the line to an end, terminating a vehicle that had begun in the 1960s. This decision may be the best illustration of Nissan's decline. I thought that the symbol of Nissan's comeback should focus around a new Z. The attachment and nostalgia that Americans felt for the 240Z could be seen by the large number of Datsun 240Z "fan clubs." One cannot overstate how precious this sort of emotional capital is. Patrick Le Quément claimed that Nissan design was among the most innovative in the world in those days. Recreating the Z would be tantamount to uncovering Nissan's genetic signature, its DNA.

No choice weighs so heavily in determining a vehicle's commercial success or failure than its design. That is why the choice of the heads of design is so important.

Before I came to Nissan, the executive who made the final decision on a model's design was the head of engineering. When I became CEO, that decision rested with me. I became the first

CEO of a car manufacturer to convene executive committee meetings on the test tracks, where we tried out the competition's cars. Before, the people at the top of Nissan weren't really engaged with its products. Nissan's key managers often rose through the ranks of personnel. Now, I don't deny that knowing how to manage others is important. But if you don't know anything about motor vehicles—if you don't know how cars are built, or what their technical characteristics are, or how long it takes to develop new models, or how the priorities line up—you can't be an effective manager of a car manufacturer, especially during a period of crisis.

Design wasn't the only area where Nissan needed to transform itself. As is frequently the case with a company on the verge of bankruptcy, Nissan's financial management left a lot to be desired.

Up until 1996, Nissan had no chief financial officer. And when one was finally appointed, he lacked the necessary experience and he didn't even have access to all the indispensable information. Nonetheless, he was charged with defining the budget and the company's financial goals. He had to do a job that rightly should have been done by the head of the company, and he had to do it without the necessary knowledge and power.

Companies in the automobile business are great consumers of capital. An assembly plant capable of producing 250,000 vehicles annually costs more than a billion dollars. The development of an entirely new model costs several hundred million dollars. But in the Japanese growth model between 1950 and 1990, the cost of money was negligible. The banks channeled Japan's vast savings to the corporations, generally at very low interest rates. The discipline of capital markets, which require a certain level of profitability from invested capital, didn't hold.

People within the company didn't act as though money was a rare and costly resource. There had always been enough of it, and it didn't cost anything, because interest rates were so low. If money isn't considered a rare resource, how can you expect a company to pay serious attention to it? If I needed money, I could get it from the bank, which also happened to be my principal shareholder. As soon as credit began to get tight, people should have started asking themselves some questions. But that didn't happen, and when the company needed money in order to keep functioning, there was no more credit. It wasn't the cost of money that exposed the limits of the system. It was the fact that money was no longer available at any cost. All of a sudden, people realized that this was a limited resource, and that led to panic.

Improving the health of Nissan's finances was a top priority. The infusion of money from Renault and the sell-off of all non-strategic stocks were the most visible signs of Nissan's new financial policy. But the company also needed a financial structure adapted to its new environment, in which Nissan's *keiretsu* networks were dismantled and market forces were allowed to work. I gave this job to Thierry Moulonguet, whom I had promoted to chief financial officer, and to his team. Their first decision called for all Nissan's financial functions, which had been delegated to the various subsidiaries, to be centralized in Tokyo.

What was costing Nissan the most wasn't the debt it had underwritten in Japan—where interest rates were quite low—but the debts it had contracted in the United States, in Mexico, and in Southeast Asia, where the company was paying staggering finance charges. One of the goals I set for the financial department from the start was the repatriation of all Nissan's debt to Japan. Today, Nissan has no debts. When I joined the company, Nissan carried a big debt in Mexico. If there was one country where a company should absolutely never have gone into debt, it was Mexico, with its astronomical interest rates and the downward spiral of the peso against the dollar. Each fluctuation meant heavy losses.

The United States was Nissan's most important market outside Japan, and I was actively involved there right from the start. I quickly realized that the position of president of Nissan America was more of a hindrance than an advantage. And it was the same in Europe. Instead of accelerating the rate of change inside the company, these positions were slowing it down. When you've got a company in decline, there are always some areas that are more affected than others. There's black, there's white, and there are several shades of gray. In Japan, where the crisis was most intense, Nissan's results had deteriorated the most. But our European organization had also deteriorated. And then there was the United States, where things were somewhat better. But, considering Nissan America's potential, it had recorded very mediocre results. Our first goal was to say to the Americans, "Don't compare yourselves to the Europeans or the Japanese; compare yourselves to your own potential. You've got a long way to go." Consequently, one of my very first decisions was to eliminate the two regional presidencies. They were replaced by four-person regional teams, which consisted of the head of marketing; the head of research and development; the person responsible for manufacturing, purchasing, and quality control; and the administrative and finance director. They're in charge of regional management and they report to a nonresident president, a member of Nissan's executive committee in Tokyo. I appointed Norio Matsumura to head the U.S. operation, and I put Patrick Pelata in charge of Europe; Japan I took for myself. (In April 2004, I took charge of North American operations, and Matsumura was put in charge of Japan.) And now, at last, we've rationalized the organization for the other countries in the world. I tried to jump over everything that looked like a wall, everything that could be seen as an obstacle to the changes I wanted. Every three months, I preside over a meeting of the regional management committees. Every quarter, we take stock of the situation. Tokyo doesn't require an exhaustive report. We told the regional managers that they were in charge, the responsibility was theirs, and that we'd make sure they found *support* in company headquarters, not handicaps. But the other side of responsibility is transparency.

They know that we want to know everything there is to know about the most important subjects. The principle is this: "If you're not transparent, you're going to have fewer responsibilities. We don't want any surprises. If you've got problems, we can discuss them. We can help you. If everything's going well, then tell us that, too, and we'll let you alone, because we have enough to do elsewhere." This spirit of responsibility and transparency has caught on well. Today, everyone in the company has a much clearer vision of what the regions' responsibilities are in relation to headquarters' responsibilities. Headquarters is responsible for finalizing and deciding strategy, for policy in regard to products and brand image, and for the choice of the top managers. But once the budgets are fixed, they're the ones who are responsible. I don't practice micromanagement. But if there's a slide in results, I react right away. We ask the managers, "What are you doing? How do you react to a situation, and when?" We're alert, we're on guard, but they're responsible.

A description of Nissan that had become commonplace in the automotive industry was "Good engineers, bad salesmen." Nissan's engineering is very strong. It's one of the bulwarks of the company, along with production. But it's a world unto itself. If you look at Nissan's weaknesses in marketing and sales and compare them to the level of its engineering, you wouldn't think that the two divisions were working for the same company.

Toyota's strength lies in the fact that most of its dealerships are independent. Toyota's dealers feel themselves engaged at every stage in the sale of Toyota's vehicles. The situation at Nissan was exactly the opposite. Its sales network was dominated by subsidiaries of Nissan. Everyone in these subsidiaries, both subordinates and directors—who often were assigned there from Nissan headquarters at the end of their careers—behaved like ordinary employees, not like entrepreneurs.

The kinds of relationships that we maintained in our Japanese sales network were exceedingly mediocre. We didn't understand their problems, and they didn't understand Nissan. We were in an absolute free-fall. The majority of the management in these subsidiaries came from Nissan, but I'm not certain that they considered themselves leaders of a team and a company, responsible for increasing Nissan's market share and making profits. Their conception of their role was more social than genuinely operational. During the course of the last three years, this situation has very much changed for the better, principally because of changes in management and because we've endeavored to establish more direct communications with our sales network. But I don't think you can bring about profound changes in these relationships without being present on the ground, without giving very detailed examples of what has to be done, without listening to problems and proposals, and without making swift, highly visible adjustments. If there's one area where the changes we are making will prove to be most important—and they haven't all been accomplished yet—it's in Nissan's distribution network in Japan. When I took over, it was the least efficient sector in the company.

To put an end to senseless geographical overlaps, more than 300 dealerships out of 3,000 were closed. The number of dealerships that were Nissan subsidiaries was reduced from more than 100 to 80, with more reductions planned. This was accomplished in part by selling some dealerships to independent operators, or by consolidating two or more operations.

The goal is to have a network imbued with the entrepreneurial spirit. However, transforming a subsidiary into an independent doesn't automatically resolve the situation, because if the independent isn't any good, than the situation can be worse than it was before. It's a question of making sure that subsidiary dealerships pass into the hands of good independent dealers, people who are real entrepreneurs. In 1999 and 2000, there weren't many entrepreneurs who were ready to invest in the Nissan sales network. And that's quite understandable. If you wanted to buy an automobile dealership, Nissan wasn't exactly the ideal choice. We had to do whatever it took to revitalize the network. That meant, in the first place, raising the bar in terms of performance and efficiency on the part of the subsidiaries, which represented about 50% of our sales network in Japan. To achieve this, we had to rely on commonsense measures: refocusing on profitability and brand image, dealing with unresolved difficulties, creating a system of quick reaction to problems. We had to interrupt the dialogue of the deaf we had going, where the sales network complained about not having good products to sell but neither the commercial organization nor the network was capable of suggesting what kind of products they thought the company should put on the market. There was a litany of reciprocal complaints, recited in a climate of general collapse. I believe that a carmaker has the sales network it deserves, and that was the case with Nissan. Since then, firmly and steadily, we're climbing back out of the hole. During the course of the next two years, I hope we're going to see a network emerge that's in much better shape than the one we inherited in 1999. We measure its progress not only by how much our market share increases and how solidly the network returns to profitability, but also by our consumer satisfaction index and by customers' purchase intent. We have to be sure that everyone who walks into a dealership receives an impression of quality and professionalism. All this can be measured, and it will allow us to demonstrate the difference between yesterday, today, and tomorrow.

In Japan, sales are largely based on the personal relationship between the seller and his customer, a relationship maintained throughout the years by house calls, after-sale service, and unbroken contact between the brand and the customer. Calculated in terms of units sold per month, a Japanese car salesman's productivity is weak in comparison to a European's or an American's. But the system has advantages as well as disadvantages. Customer brand loyalty is very strong, and that's why Nissan's steady decline was of such concern. It was imperative that we give Nissan's salesmen back their desire to sell.

The key to everything, of course, was the launching of new products. The Nissan Revival Plan's product planning called for twelve new models to appear at diminishing intervals over a three-year period. The first two years, 2000 and 2001, were difficult. Before the company could even think about reconquering lost territory, the first priority was to stop the erosion of Nissan's market share. We achieved this in 2001, at which time Nissan had a share of just under 18% of passenger cars in Japan, excluding mini-cars. The real turning point was to come in March 2002, when Nissan launched the new March in Japan. The March was the first Nissan vehicle built on a platform that was shared by Renault. Moreover, the March was an entry-level vehicle, and it appeared at a moment when Japan's economic difficulties were dragging down the automobile market across the board. The new little Nissan was going to compete against the best-selling models of our two chief competitors, the Toyota Vitz and the Honda Fit.

Three months after the launch, we were on the way to winning our bet. We had to increase production to 17,500 units per month, well beyond our initial goal of 8,000 per month. At the end of 2002, the March stood in third place on the list of the biggest-selling cars in Japan.

The other major change was our decision to enter a sector of the market unique to Japan: mini-cars, small vehicles with engine capacity of less than 650 cubic centimeters. Mini-cars accounted for fully a third of private car sales in Japan. The Moco, manufactured for Nissan by Suzuki Motor, turned a new page in Nissan's history. The March/Micra was also a big winner for us. At our launch, we sold an entire month's production in a week. Dealers want to work for a make of car whose products are in demand. When they saw the new 350Z, they were excited. They knew that having a car like that in their showrooms would attract a lot of young people and a lot of automobile enthusiasts, who would be potential customers for other products. Products are events; their arrival is anticipated, coordinated, focused on; they're supported by a strong advertising campaign and a good flow of information. That's what the sellers want: a project, a strategy, product planning that makes sense.

When it came to the American sales network, I got personally involved. The automobile market in the United States is controlled by powerful independent dealers who cover a town, a county, even one or several states. They often handle several makes of cars, and their fidelity to a manufacturer is mostly a function of the bottom line. Nissan's American distribution network had suffered a great deal from its lack of attractive products and from the discounts that the decline of the brand forced the company to give. These discounts were costing us $1,000 per vehicle compared to equivalent models by our competitors.

My experience in America has proved to be a valuable asset in defining priorities—knowing what's done and not done, knowing what's acceptable and what's unacceptable. I often travel to the United States and participate in dealers' meetings there. When the revival plan was announced, our U.S. dealers were skeptical. But now they're very motivated, because everything is on the table in plain sight. They can see that we've realized the goals we set in 1999: We've returned to profitability, we've reinvested in technology and in our American production capacity, we're rolling out new models. The Altima is a hit in the United States. We build 20,000 a month, and we sell every unit we produce, practically without incentives. We entered new segments of the market with the Murano crossover SUV and the Quest minivan. Our new Mississippi plant has been up and running since the spring of 2003. Our Canton products—the Titan truck, Armada SUV, and Infiniti QX56—put us in the highly profitable full-size vehicle segments. Our American dealers, Nissan as well as Infiniti, our luxury brand, have made a full comeback. They're seeing sales growth and increased profit margins. They see a company that's investing in its future, that is working on our brand image, our visual identity. And they incorporate the company's improved image into their own consciousness.

Today, people don't talk about Nissan as a company in trouble anymore. On the contrary, they wonder how far Nissan can go.

CHAPTER 16

A NEW CULTURE

Although our initial intention wasn't to change Nissan's culture, the fact is that the company's culture is constantly evolving. We didn't want to make changes for the sake of change; we wanted to make them for the sake of performance. In every step we've taken, we've been very careful not to institute changes that haven't been based strictly on the advantages they give us, the progress in company performance that they contribute to. We didn't come to Japan as missionaries. We came to put Nissan back on a performance curve more in keeping with its potential. If we come across certain cultural elements—even if we don't agree with them, even if we don't like them—we leave them alone, unless we think that modifying them is indispensable to improving the company's results. We strive to make the minimum number of changes necessary for achieving maximum performance. We accepted Nissan's culture and its current practices just as we found them. We change only those elements that are linked to Nissan's problems.

In the beginning, our approach was quite modest, even if the changes we instituted were very important later on. What was important wasn't resolving all the dysfunctions in the company; it was detecting the most crucial ones and dealing with them. We couldn't afford to spread ourselves too thinly. We had to know when to leave things alone. Take the period from 1990 to 2000. When I look at Toyota and Honda on the one hand, and Nissan on the other, it's obvious that there were winners and losers. It's stupid to pretend otherwise. In profitability, in market share, there were winners and losers. Once you've admitted that, the next necessary step is to explain the reasons for it. When a company has been winning over a long period of time, that's not the result of chance. It's the result of a strategy and of a certain quality of management. If the loser fails to recognize his situation, he can't recover. A fundamental requirement for any recovery is an admission on the part of the company that it's made some mistakes, that its product, its design, its technology aren't up to the proper level. And that its management isn't, either! In Nissan's case, its decline, its looming crisis, were inscribed in its results, month after month, year after year. And yet the management of the company had been unable to react until it was at a crisis point.

Nissan had gradually developed a culture in which the standard response to problems was "It's not me, it's someone else." If the company was in trouble, it was always the fault of other people. The sales department complained about product planning, thus effectively knocking the ball into the engineering department's court. Engineering blamed finance. Nissan Europe accused Tokyo, and vice versa. The root of the problem was that the areas of executive responsibility were vague.

In a typically bureaucratic move, Nissan had even diluted managers' responsibilities by creating a whole corps of "advisers" and "coordinators." These people had no direct operational functions, but they were placed alongside managers on the ground. Originally, such advisers were active in the foreign subsidiaries of Japanese companies, facilitating the dissemination of Japanese "best practices" in management or production. Growing familiarity with these practices had eliminated the usefulness of the advisers, but they stayed in place all the same. The only result they produced was to undermine the authority of the people with operational responsibilities. We eliminated this function, gave all those who fitted such roles direct responsibilities, and put them back to work.

The role of "advisers" in the big Japanese companies exemplifies the ossification of principles or values that originally were quite positive. The respect due to "elders" in Confucian societies, the role of the master, the *sensei*, in the transmission of experience and knowledge, the desire to be gentle with people who are at the end of their careers and who must be eased out slowly—all these are worthwhile, perhaps even useful notions. But they invite abuses. How many Japanese companies are still carrying the financial burden of their "senior advisers," generally former CEOs and presidents, with offices, secretaries, and chauffeured automobiles? The result is a network of gray heads that has transformed the Japanese business world, little by little, into a venerable gerontocracy. Another example of a practice that's injurious to performance is the system of advancement by seniority. Obviously, we couldn't ask the entire management for significant contributions to the development of company performance if we didn't judge people essentially on their ability to contribute. If we wanted to make a qualitative leap, if we wanted to effect a rapid change in the level of performance, we couldn't maintain the seniority system. We had to be logical. We were going to judge our people according to their contribution to the NRP. Their performance would be decisive in determining their salaries as well as their professional future. Age and seniority were no longer going to be the determining factors in a career; they'd be elements to take into consideration after an examination of the individual's performance. In this area, we brought about a really significant change.

The abandonment of the system of advancement by seniority had major implications for Japanese companies. In the traditional model, a young graduate was recruited as soon as he or she left the university, often through the recommendations of alumni of the same alma mater. The new employee's beginning salary was low, precisely because the seniority system guaranteed raises that came with the regularity of a metronome until one reached retirement age. The connection between performance and promotion was practically nonexistent. This system discouraged individual initiative, nurtured blind, hierarchical subordination, and fostered cliques and behind-the-scenes turf battles over the delegation of responsibilities.

In my view, one of the prime responsibilities of any CEO consists in preparing future leaders to succeed to top-level positions (including my own) in the company. That may seem self-evident, but it's far from being the rule. And not only in Japan.

I've seen a raft of European and American companies whose bosses were more interested in protecting their positions at the top than in the future of the enterprise. And that doesn't happen just in the business world. But some people are profoundly conscious of their company's interests, and those are the ones I want to talk to. I'm not going to waste my time with someone whose sole concern is his personal interest. When you consider Nissan's experience, you can see that there's a way for a top manager to show he deserves the responsibilities he's been given while at the same time helping the company get back on its feet, and that way involves selecting people who are capable of opening the doors to the future. And there's only one way of accomplishing this: You allow people to prove themselves.

Is there such a thing as a born leader? I don't think so. Many people have an aptitude for leadership; there are more of them than you might think. They get sorted out according to the opportunities they have to exercise and develop that aptitude. If they're in the right place at the right time, they get their first chance, they take up a challenge, and they win. Then along comes a second, and they win again. Their self-confidence grows, and that's the way you form leaders. Of course, some are lost along the way, some wilt under fire, some fail or even collapse. But if you offer such chances on a large enough scale, you'll be able to identify a sufficient number of talented people to ensure that your company has a very vigorous leadership for a long time to come.

General Electric is a pretty interesting case. Many people have failed at GE, but it's certainly generated a lot of leaders, not because the company has always chosen the most talented, but because it has developed them. GE's directors have set conditions that allow people to dare, and they've accepted failure as part of promoting success. And in the end, they've succeeded. Jack Welch enjoyed the luxury of having several possible successors, not because he was lucky but because he'd done everything he could to be in that situation when the time came for him to retire. Every company leader has the responsibility to do the same.

Over the long term, no power can stand against the failure to perform. When a company's not performing, that should sound loud alarm bells, at least for those managers determined to keep it from sinking. Some people consider preserving their own power more important than the future of the company.

At Nissan, the crisis we underwent completely changed the rules of the game. Gently, gradually, without drama but also without compromise, an entire generation of top managers, worn down by Nissan's years of struggle, was eased out of power. And a new generation was offered the chance to control the company's destiny.

It's imperative for a company to prepare its future managers. You can't prepare them by leaving them at company headquarters to work in administrative functions. You prepare them by sending them to the most difficult places. A certain number of them will fail, but the ones who emerge will provide the breeding ground for tomorrow's leaders. Tomorrow's leaders get their training by dealing with today's challenges. You have to take the ones with the most potential and send them where the action is. That way, you achieve two ends: You get the problem taken care of, and you get a manager who's grown through experience. Leaders are formed in the fire of experience. It's up to the head of the company to prepare a new generation and to send them to hot spots as part of their training. He must prepare for a smooth transition by training people, guiding them, pushing them forward, but not too hard. Then, from among them, he must choose the successful ones, the future managers and directors, the ones he has confidence in, not because they're someone's protégé but because they've faced difficult tasks and accomplished them. All the people who've been promoted recently at Nissan have been people we've discovered in our own ranks. We've let them take some chances, they've handled them successfully, and now they're being given greater responsibilities. This is an ongoing process, and today nothing stands in its way.

Another practice that's very Japanese and very dear to Nissan's heart is lifetime employment. I don't think the notion of employment for life is intrinsically mistaken—it's not a bad thing in itself. It's a goal. A company that needs the loyalty of its employees must demonstrate a loyalty toward them, as well. However, lifetime employment can't be a guarantee. It's an objective to be pursued continually, but it's basically dependent on the capacity of the company to conduct the pursuit. Even in Japan, the only companies capable of guaranteeing lifetime employment are the ones with the highest levels of performance.

When a company's in a deteriorating situation, one of the first things it does is to try steering around the lifetime-employment requirement. The company sends people to work for its suppliers. It sends others to its dealers, then to other companies, throwing in salary cuts along the way. It pretends to be fulfilling the guarantee of lifetime employment, but that's just a ruse. In our approach, I don't think of lifetime employment in the same way I think of advancement by seniority. I think the seniority system is counterproductive; it damages performance. By contrast, I think it's a good idea for a company to demonstrate its loyalty to its employees, to the people who constitute the company, even if it's not realistic to elevate that practice into an immutable law. We're headed there, we're working toward that goal, we don't treat the matter lightly. We recognize that it's a worthy goal, but we also recognize that it's very difficult to attain.

When we stopped promoting people on the basis of seniority, it meant, in effect, that we'd be hiring new people at higher entry-level salaries, and that bonuses or raises could be more considerable and more frequent. It wasn't the fixed part, the base salaries, that grew so much, it was the variable part, and that variable part was linked to company performance. This way, you don't add to your fixed costs. If the company performs well, then employees benefit from that; if it performs badly, the variable part of their salaries is reduced accordingly. So part of your salary—at least if you're in management—is tied to company performance. For Nissan's top managers, the variable part of their remuneration, exclusive of stock options, can be as high as 40% of their total salary.

To establish the variable part of an employee's remuneration, there are two possible systems: rewards or incentives. In the first case, you work all year, and at the end of the year, your boss signals his appreciation and raises your salary. It's not really clear on what basis or according to what precise criteria your raise is quantified—it's entirely up to your boss. We don't practice that method. Instead, we use a very simple system of incentives. At the beginning of the fiscal year, on April 1, we allocate the incentives for that year. Before the year starts, our managers know what criteria they're going to be judged on and what they'll receive for the realization of this or that goal. There are many clearly stated, quantitative criteria, while others—as few as possible—are qualitative. In some areas, you can't have solely quantitative criteria.

At the end of the fiscal year, management only has to do the accounts. Have the goals been reached? Yes or no? There can be debates about whether market conditions, the exchange rate, or whether the work of other sectors has helped or not, but there can't be two opinions about whether or not a quantified goal has been realized. This reduces the field of discussion, and that's why I much prefer an incentive system to a system of rewards. The incentive system puts limits on subjective evaluations of an employee's contribution. If someone has reached all his goals, you can hardly tell him he won't get the maximum increase. If someone hasn't reached all his goals, you have to try to understand why, and you may arrive at a qualified judgment. I try to make sure that people don't wind up justifying everything. What makes this system more acceptable is that the rules are known in advance. I wanted to set up the most transparent system possible, so people would accept it.

In Japan, the notion of fairness is very important. I respect fairness, but it has to be linked to an employee's contribution, not to individual persons. You can't say you're being fair if you treat everyone the same way, without distinguishing between someone who makes a big contribution, someone who makes an average contribution, and the person whose contribution is negligible. I don't think of that as fairness. It's certainly not fair to the company's customers or its shareholders or its other employees. So we've made the idea of fairness tilt more toward performance. And we moved away from focusing on efforts to focusing on results.

Japanese companies have gradually developed a culture of "presence." People would always work incredibly long hours at their desks and receive overtime. "The company" expected its faithful employees to give up their holidays voluntarily. The excessive amount of time that Japanese workers spent in their offices was the price they paid for their lack of productivity, which was often connected with the way the company functioned and the way its decisions were made. Such overtime hours were catastrophic for many corporate budgets . . . as well as for the family life of many an office worker.

The fact that someone works a lot is less important than the fact that he gets results. Some people work all the time without ever getting good results. In my case, no one really cares whether or not I work sixteen hours a day. I'm not paid according to the number of hours I spend in my office but according to the results I produce for the company. Results are what are important, especially at the management level. We're passing from a culture of presence to a culture of efficiency. This obliges people to rely on their teams, because results generally correspond to the quality of teamwork. The notion of effort is much more focused on individuals.

At Nissan, the acceptance of these changes proceeded from three key elements: the acknowledgment that the company had no other choice, the company's rapid return to better results, and, finally, the fact that Japan itself was ready for such a revolution, even if it wasn't always conducted so boldly everywhere in the country. In Nissan's case, the unions accepted the revolution, but it's obviously easier to do that when the company's growing stronger and its employees see the variable part of their salaries steadily increasing. The real test will come the day the company begins to perform less well and the variable part decreases. However, all things considered, the advantages of this system far outweigh its disadvantages. It induces people to take a very concrete, very immediate interest in improving company performance.

During the wage negotiations, known as *shunto* (the unions' spring offensive for wages, often roundly condemned), while most corporations, including Toyota, were freezing base wages or limiting increases to a strict minimum, I decided to accede to the demands of Nissan's unions in their entirety.

From the start, I'd pointed out that the Nissan Revival Plan wasn't in place solely for the benefit of our customers or our shareholders, but also for our employees. It's easy to say such a thing, but when you can give a clear signal and confirm your words by actions, then you have to do so. I didn't decide to accept the unions' 2002 wage demands, for example, by way of provoking Japanese industry. I found myself in a situation in which I was convinced that it was imperative to give everything I could. When we debated the question, I told my team that I didn't see how we could say no. It's true that all this took place within an economic context that was rather difficult for Japan, but the unions' demands were reasonable. There wasn't any financial disagreement. It was a question of saying to all of our employees, "You supported the plan, you played your part, you participated in a critical stage in the life of the company, and the company can't refuse to give you what you're asking for." Moreover, the chairman of Toyota's board of directors said in the end that Nissan's situation was special. Basically, he said that Nissan hadn't raised salaries and wages when everyone else was doing so; that we were giving raises now that our results had improved. I was quite happy to be a special case, but I hadn't acted to influence the actions of other companies; I acted out of conviction. However, since we were the only company to act this way, we were very conspicuous.

It would be going too far to claim that Japanese public opinion understood and accepted all these momentous changes. At the general meeting of Nissan's shareholders in June 2002, a minor shareholder, a veteran of many combative interventions, rose to protest the board's decision to increase the directors' profit share by 50% when dividends had risen by only 14%. I was away for family reasons, so the task of justifying a bonus in recompense for our spectacular recovery fell to Yoshikazu Hanawa. He pointed out that Nissan's shareholders had already benefited from the recovery: The value of their stock had doubled. In a similar fashion, granting stock options is still relatively rare in Japan and has not always been understood or treated approvingly by the media. However, for me, stock options play an integral part in a whole ensemble of measures designed to improve company performance.

The idea that people have the ability to get richer—relatively speaking, at least—is starting to be accepted within the company. People are quite happy when they receive their options. Some get more than others, according to the responsibilities they exercise and the risks they're taking. Options are a supplement. They don't create motivation, but they reinforce it.

In the case of Japan, there's a second concern. Pension systems are in a very difficult situation today. You can't expect people to agree to spend the most productive years of their lives working for your company when they know its pension system is in total disarray. The stock options will allow them to take care of at least part of their needs after they retire. It's a fundamentally sound concept. Instead of falling back on the company, they can rely on their work, the work of their team, and their results to provide for their legitimate needs. You must realize that some Nissan executives have spent years with the company, accepting salary reductions, able to save little or nothing. By contrast, the stock-options system is very sound; it tells them that they can make a lot of money by making a strong contribution to the company's recovery—enough money to resolve the potential problems of retirement. In the course of 2003, 900 Nissan people profited from this system. That may sound like a drop in the bucket in comparison to the company's 125,000 employees, but those are the 900 people who exercise the greatest responsibilities.

Almost from the start, our management team made a serious effort to persuade its employees and investors to participate financially in the revival of the company. But this was a difficult task. Discouraged by the collapse of the Japanese stock market after the bursting of the speculative bubble in the 1990s, individual investors deserted the market to place their nest eggs in bank deposits or postal accounts. And the Japanese banks, which had traditionally been large shareholders in Japanese corporations, began to reduce their holdings of industrial stocks. As a result, by 2002 more than two-thirds of Nissan's stock was in the hands of non-Japanese investors. Above the 44.4% held by Renault, another quarter of the capital was owned by foreign (mostly American) investment or retirement funds. The shares owned by the Japanese banks had fallen to zero. Small Japanese shareholders accounted for some 6% of the stock, and the balance was held by financial institutions.

To facilitate the acquisition of Nissan stock by our employees, we offered at the general shareholders' meeting the opportunity to vote for a proposition to lower the minimum number of shares that could be purchased at one time—from one thousand to one hundred. We wanted to encourage not only our employees but also private investors to purchase smaller blocks of Nissan stock. For a thousand shares of Nissan stock, you had to put down a million yen. If the minimum package costs one-tenth that, it becomes a lot more accessible.

CHAPTER 17

MAKING THE ALLIANCE LIVE

W e're entering a century that's going to be increasingly marked by globalization, like it or not. It's a fact. Barriers are falling and all sorts of exchanges are proliferating—economic, financial, cultural, human. People no longer want to be walled up inside a closed society. They want to make exchanges, see things, travel; they want to consider the whole world as their domain, not just their country, their city, or their village. And that's going to start happening faster and faster. All you have to do is observe the younger generation, which is much more international in its interests and attitudes than the one that preceded it. However, besides this openness to globalization, there's also the desire on the part of people to maintain a sense of national identity. That desire makes its presence known everywhere, sometimes in a positive way, sometimes in a negative way. As far as I'm concerned, globalization and respect for national identity must go hand in hand. Your identity includes your country of origin, your culture of origin, its history, its language.

What goes for individuals applies to corporations as well. Every day, more and more, their market is the world. Protectionism is continually losing ground. The growth of global exchange has been the principal engine of development. With the end of the Cold War and the opening of such large, previously closed markets as China and India, almost the entire planet now participates in the international division of labor.

To say that a company has a cultural heritage and a history connected to such and such a nationality is fine with me. But before long, only regional or local companies will be able to define themselves in terms of nationality. Corporations can be Japanese, say, or French, and be proud of it, but I think identifying themselves that way will become less and less common in the future. At Nissan, there's a Japanese culture, Japanese history, and most of the executives are Japanese; it's a reality. But all the same, the future will belong to the globalized companies that seek to adopt the best practices and to open themselves to the whole world, while at the same time trying to preserve their identity. I don't think one can be open to the world and deeply nationalistic at the same time. It seems obvious to me that we have to change the parameters of the issue. We must indeed preserve our identity, but the identity in question will be a corporate identity, not a national identity anymore. Admittedly, national identity still determines a significant proportion of a company's identity. But if you limit yourself to that, you condemn yourself to stagnation.

Today, all the meetings of Nissan's executive committee are conducted in English. Obviously, there are other meetings where we use translators, but many people in the company can communicate in English. Requiring the use of English was made easier for me by the fact that I'm neither of Anglo-Saxon extraction nor a product of Anglo-Saxon culture. I've got no cultural predisposition to favor English. All my education was in French, and French is still the language I speak best. But we chose English because we had to be objective and acknowledge that when a Chinese person gets together with a German, a Frenchman, an American, and a Japanese, there's not much chance that they're going to speak French, or Chinese, or anything other than English. Learning English isn't a cultural notion. It's like buying a software package to manage your electronic mail. You download it into your computer because you can't communicate without it. We've made English an everyday language. It was a management decision—we gave ourselves a tool to help us communicate with people who work for the same company but come from different cultures. Nissan has made a lot of progress. Obviously, there are numerous sectors of the company where people don't speak a word of English because they have no need to. People working at a Japanese dealership couldn't care less about English. But those who work at company headquarters, especially the top executives, realize that they need to speak English. They're learning the language and starting to participate. It's not perceived as a burden.

What made this process easier at Nissan was that the Japanese realized that learning English was as difficult for the French as it was for them. When conversations were conducted, they noticed that the French weren't necessarily better prepared than they were to speak English. The French use Gallicisms; they speak with heavy accents. The upshot was that neither side had more of an inferiority complex than the other. It wouldn't have been as comfortable a situation if Renault had forced everyone to speak English because the Renault people were better at it than the Japanese. And things would certainly have been different between Americans or Britons and Japanese.

For experienced executives, whether in Tokyo or in Billancourt, going back to school hasn't always been easy. But the two companies put in place programs to learn English, along with incentives for participating in them. The progress, in just a few years, has been spectacular. There was the suspicion among managers that those who spoke English would be considered more valuable than those who didn't, but it's just an undeniable fact: Speaking English is a real asset. Still, we try our best not to ignore people who don't speak English, just for that reason. On the other hand, you can obviously show yourself to best advantage if you can communicate easily. It's an advantage for both groups, Japanese and French.

It was the Alliance that brought about this change, but this was a change that would have been necessary whether there was an

Alliance or not, because Nissan is a global enterprise, active in 192 countries, with operations in North America, Europe, Asia, the Middle East, and so on. One of the first problems brought up by people working for Nissan outside Japan was that there were so few people in the company's Tokyo headquarters who could speak English. When there was something to discuss with them, communication was very difficult. You couldn't make a telephone call or send an e-mail. A problem like this affects the company as a whole, especially its ability to react swiftly, and it limits cross-functional work. English is a tool, reduced for our purposes to its true dimension: a tool for globalization, for communication, and for cross-functionality. And our people have to approach it that way, just as one learns math or physics.

· · ·

Learning to communicate is one thing. For Renault and Nissan, learning to live together is more difficult. This is a job that requires a daily effort. As with a couple, there must be a clear definition of the rules and a good deal of attention paid to the other partner. The Alliance is making progress because it respects individual and cultural identities. Respect for identities can't be accomplished passively. It's deliberate and active. How can we improve performance within the framework of the Alliance and maintain respect for our separate identities at the same time? How can we tear down walls, build bridges, and maintain our individual sense of identity? Preserving one's identity implies a certain level of self-affirmation in dealing with others, but exchanging with others implies a willingness to blend with them. And we're subject to both impulses. We're going to have to respect both of them, whether within a single company or within the framework of the global economy, and this necessity is absolute within the framework of the Alliance. The essential first step in working together successfully is mutual respect. We can accept globalization all the more readily if our individual identities are preserved and affirmed.

I can't judge with absolute certainty whether the French and the Japanese, or Renault and Nissan, were meant for each other. But it's obvious that French culture, although it's a strong culture with a powerful sense of its own identity, is also a culture that's quite permeable. In France, you start learning very young to take an interest in different cultures. People there are curious about what's different, about what's unlike themselves. I don't mean that someone who comes from a less permeable culture is necessarily doomed to failure, because at the end of the day, everything comes down to the individual. Culture and education help you, support you, shape you. But companies are made up of human beings, and so are their successes or their failures. French culture, because it's so permeable, facilitates establishing connections. As for Japan, it seems to me it's a country that's both open and closed at the same time. In a discussion with Shiro Nakamura, our head of design, we were talking about what it was that made up the essence of Nissan. We talked about Japanese culture. He gave me some very simple examples of ways in which Japan is simultaneously open and closed. Written Japanese uses three distinct systems—*kanji*, *hiragana*, and *katakana*—all of which have different origins. This doesn't suggest a closed culture. He showed me some examples of very simple, very airy architecture, and beside it some photographs of Shinjuku, where the scene is variegated, full of color, and extremely complex. And both styles are part of Japan. If you observe Japan with an eye for examples of how closed it is, you'll see it closed. But if you look for its open side, you'll find a lot of openness. Without being naïve, I always try to look for Japan's openness, and I've never been disappointed.

Inside the Alliance, there are some tendencies that are, in my opinion, harmful to the Alliance, and they can be found on both sides. For example, some people think they can rush things along. As far as I'm concerned, such attitudes are harmful; they destroy value. Now, we're creators of value. The success of the Alliance is based on the fact that we pay a lot of attention at all times to controlling tendencies, on one side and on the other, that could destroy value.

When Nissan was at death's door, Renault management was prudent enough to resist the temptation to exploit the imbalance of power. Louis Schweitzer's conduct was diametrically opposed to Jürgen Schrempp's, who later acknowledged that the offer of a "merger between equals" made by Daimler to Chrysler was more symbolic than actual. Renault never took advantage of Nissan. For its part, Nissan has proved itself a worthy object of Renault's hopes and has even surpassed those hopes. It's a historical fact.

At first, the exchange of practical experience was pretty much one-way, from Renault to Nissan. Now that's changing. There's a movement of people from Nissan to Renault, particularly in such areas as manufacturing, quality control, and engineering. The people who've come from France to work for Nissan in Japan aren't going to stay for life. Their repatriation will greatly enhance Renault; the people involved will have gone through a unique experience in dramatic circumstances. There will be a second wave, and then a third, of executives from Renault who'll come to Tokyo to work for Nissan and of people from Nissan who'll go to Renault. This continual movement will be very valuable. Considering the nature of the Alliance and the way its future is shaping up, it's clear that the Renault people with Nissan experience and the Nissan people with Renault experience are precious assets. As we develop synergies in every area, it will be to our advantage to have executives available to us who know the other company well. We must broaden our exchanges, but we must exercise moderation in doing so.

Let me give you an example. Within the framework of the huge X-84 program launched by Renault to replace the Mégane vehicle with the Mégane II—the first Alliance model to be built on its new manufacturing platform C—setting up the fabrication of the doors and roofs has been entrusted to Nissan. The work is being done in Renault's plants in Douai, France, and Palencia, Spain, and it's being carried out under the direct responsibility of Nissan engineers brought to Europe from Japan. Today, assembly personnel in all Renault's factories systematically attend "dexterity schools," inspired by Nissan's training methods and conducted by training staff sent from Nissan.

The exchanges of specialists began right away. Nissan needed a management renewal; on the other hand, it had plenty of technical experts who could help Renault. As time passed, the exchanges necessarily became more balanced. In the future, there will probably be people who start their careers with Renault, transfer over to Nissan, and then go back to Renault, and the same thing will happen from the other direction. Kazumasa Katoh, the head of powertrain engineering at Renault, is a fine professional. He didn't go to France in the first wave; he went in an exchange that Renault wanted, and I was careful to send them a highly qualified executive. And there will be others. We start off talking about filling needs. What are the areas where the partner needs this or that? Next, we identify the people who have that expertise. The goal is to prepare top-level Alliance executives who are equally at ease in both companies. In the end, Nissan's executive committee will still have a distinctly Japanese aspect, and Renault's will still be strongly tinged with French. But each of them, I believe, will bring in people of diverse nationalities. What we're aiming for isn't to choose people according to their nationalities but to select the best people for each company. And there are fewer candidates than you might think. There's seldom an abundance of choices for the positions of greatest responsibility.

One of the great challenges that Renault has faced in its globalization is the fact that a part of its management still sees itself as exclusively French. It goes without saying that French culture is very important in the culture of the company, and again, we mustn't lose sight of that fact. But we can't stop there. It's interesting to learn that Toyota believes they're going to become more and more American. I take them very seriously. They're asking themselves some fundamental questions. For example, if a corporation is "strictly Japanese," how much of a handicap does that represent? I believe they've put their finger on the problem. I'm convinced that if General Motors and Ford are having difficulties today, it's because they haven't become truly global corporations. They have remained too American. They realize most of their profits in the United States. They seem unable to make satisfactory, stable profits elsewhere—not in Europe, not in Latin America, and not in Asia. What we're on the way to understanding is that tomorrow's winners, at least those in the automobile industry, will be those that are truly global, capable of according equal importance to all markets. You can't treat certain markets as though they're secondary. That way of operating is over. Tomorrow's company will be the one that assumes a global character without losing its identity. This won't be easy to do. But the companies that succeed in doing it will create the most value and the most wealth, and they'll be the ones that wind up on top.

I'm convinced that Nissan, through the Renault-Nissan Alliance, will have a competitive advantage in this regard in the future: a multicultural dimension. Toyota estimates that it has the size to develop its own model and aim for 15% of the global market. While Nissan was dismantling its *keiretsu* network, Toyota chose the opposite path, gradually strengthening its ties (including its capital relationships) with the ten enterprises that constitute the "Toyota family," such as Denso, a manufacturer of automotive parts and equipment, Daihatsu, a mini-car manufacturer, and the truckmaker Hino. When necessary, Toyota knows how to extend beyond its closed circle; for example, in 2001 it reached an accord with PSA Peugeot Citroën to build a joint-venture plant in the Czech Republic that will manufacture small, low-priced vehicles for the European market. But in its culture, its management style, the makeup of its leadership, and even the influence of its founding family, Toyota remains the archetype of the traditional large Japanese corporation. Honda, on the other hand, is alone against the rest, proud of its technology, and fierce in its defense of its dearly acquired independence. Other Japanese manufacturers have entered into the orbit of one or another of the great foreign manufacturers. But I believe none of these relationships offers prospects equal to those of the Renault-Nissan Alliance. Mazda is too small to significantly change Ford; Suzuki, Isuzu, and Subaru are even smaller in comparison with their partner, General Motors.

How many Americans are on Honda's executive committee? There's a difference between a multicultural enterprise and an international enterprise. It's hard to be multicultural without being international, but the reverse isn't true. What's going to distinguish Nissan from the other Japanese carmakers is that it's going to become the most global, culturally speaking, of the great Japanese companies. Collaborations between Honda and other manufacturers are rare; we, on the other hand, spend all our time collaborating. We collaborate with Suzuki and with Ford, and we have an alliance with Renault. We're crossing cultures and experiences. In my opinion, that's an advantage for the future. The world that's emerging depends on interrelationships. Nissan is building a culture that's well adapted to this new world. At the top levels of the company, we can't think in specifically Japanese or French terms any longer. We have to ask ourselves, "What are the best practices in France, the best practices in Japan, the best practices at Renault and Nissan?" And we must be able to adopt those practices without hesitation or culture shock. Nissan's cross-fertilization and its multicultural dimension are elements that are very important for its future. Nissan has been revitalized faster and more thoroughly than expected. The coverage of the world market has increased significantly, with each partner drawing on the other's strengths. Renault has supported Nissan in Latin America and Europe, while Renault has leaned on Nissan in

Mexico, Asia, and the Pacific. The structure of the Alliance has been remodeled, its capital relationships reinforced, and the integration of its functions (purchasing, information technologies) accentuated. This evolution will continue, at a rhythm dictated by the goal of performance.

There's a common structure in purchasing, and another in information technology. And we'll surely create several more. But they'll always involve support functions, and they'll always be based on common sense. By contrast, we'll never run the risk of blurring the distinctions between identities. In the case of our brand names, that's obvious. But the same holds true for the identities of the two companies, because blurring distinctions would do a great deal of damage to value and to motivation, and the whole object of what we're doing is to increase motivation, to build a sense of belonging. This wouldn't be compatible with anything resembling a merger or an amalgamation. The fact that Renault is a part of Nissan's identity and Nissan is a part of Renault's is evident from the fact that nobody today thinks of Renault without thinking of Nissan and vice versa. The two companies are seen as different but at the same time bound together. We want a partnership founded on a quest for performance, not on power relationships. After several years, we don't have any particular conflicts; there aren't any misunderstandings. And I'm not just talking about the top—ask people at the lower levels and you'll get the same response. There are occasional outbursts of temper or regrets that things aren't moving faster, but nothing serious. Renault's motivation is strong, and Nissan's is equally so.

Nissan's performance has reached a level that no one could have imagined only a few years ago. This proves that the Alliance and the way the two companies work together have met with general acceptance from top to bottom. Nonetheless, observers and analysts still regard this totally new construction with a certain skepticism. Some people distrust the sincerity of a discourse that describes a balanced alliance functioning on the basis of mutual respect for identities. They say it's too good to be true. Many observers see the Alliance as a relationship between strength and weakness, a power relationship. Some looked at Renault-Nissan in the beginning and speculated as to when the big bad wolf of Billancourt would come out of the woods. Now it's rather the reverse. People think that Nissan is bigger and stronger than before, and from that they conclude that there must be an imbalance in the Alliance from our end. That's all wrong. We're not in a power relationship. We've formed an alliance. It has some advantages and some drawbacks, some successes and some insufficiencies, and sometimes things are more or less easy for one or the other of the partners, but our relation is a partnership. If the markets are skeptical about us, well, that's understandable. Analysts love black-and-white situations. They think in terms of power. The only response we can give them is to keep on going the way we're headed. We're building as we go, but we're building with clear convictions and on firm foundations. The alliance between Renault and Nissan is a unique coupling, a completely new chapter in contemporary industrial history.

In mid-2004, Nissan's capitalization, about 41 billion euros, represented 2.1 times that of Renault. Theoretically, a corporate predator could pick up 100% of Renault and 44% of Nissan for the equivalent of Renault's capitalization.

But a hostile-takeover attempt aimed at Renault could only occur in theory, because the French state owns so much Renault stock. The government's not about to beat a retreat, and that attitude won't change as long as Renault isn't decently valued. When the valuation gives an absurd result—when you can use it to declare that Renault is worth less than its Nissan stock—then you know that situation can't last. You can't ever protect yourself completely from a takeover attempt. The market states that whoever has the financial means to buy a company, any company at all, can do so. The important point is to assure that your company is valued at its fair price. Frankly, I don't believe that's the case with Renault right now. Someday, if Renault no longer has a principal shareholder, there may be a question of a takeover bid. But today, there's still a principal shareholder—the French state. And Nissan now has a 15% share of Renault's capital stock.

The equilibrium of the Alliance will rest on the performance of the two companies. I think Renault has a great deal of potential. I thought so when I joined the company in 1996, and history has shown I was right. In a few years, though we haven't come as far as we could, we've come a long way. There was a big difference between Renault in 1996 and Renault in 1999. You can judge the difference according to a whole list of criteria, both subjective and objective. Since that time, Renault has stalled a little. But, obviously, Renault has made a huge investment in Nissan, an investment in money, human resources, and time, in order to develop the Alliance. And you can't make a double profit from that investment, so Renault has had to pay the cost. Considering Nissan's recovery, the fact that Renault has a 44% share of its profits seems only just. It wouldn't be fair to emphasize Nissan's recovery and leave Renault out of consideration. Many of Renault's resources have gone into that recovery. Nissan's intrinsic performance can be evaluated such as it is, but any account of Renault's intrinsic performance has to include its 44% share in Nissan.

Logically, the aim of the Alliance is to cover the entire world with a minimum of duplication. We want to avoid making the same effort twice. If Renault were alone, the question of its return to the American market would be vexed and insoluble. It's impossible to build a global enterprise without a presence in the United States. But that's not Renault's immediate priority. Renault is moving into the Mercosur in Brazil, it's operating in Mexico, it's in a pitched battle in Europe; it's expanding into Eastern Europe and Russia, and the Renault-Samsung accord has given it a bridgehead in Asia. But if you look at the Alliance as a whole, you see things from a different angle. Today, one the Alliance's top priorities is to reinforce Nissan's presence in the United States. Nissan had 4% of the United States market in 2001. We are aiming for 6.2% in 2004. That will represent an improvement of more than 50%. Only when Nissan reaches its potential in North America will it be the time to reopen the question of Renault's return there. Given the fact that the American market is much more profitable than the other markets, Nissan necessarily brings in more than Renault. If the Japanese automobile manufacturers today are intrinsically more profitable than their European rivals, that's due in large part to their presence in North America. We have to accept it. When Renault formed its alliance with Nissan, it effectively guaranteed itself a market share in the United States. To say that Renault has no corporate presence in North America is inaccurate. Renault owns 44% of a company that's well established and profitable in the United States. If you considered the two companies as competitors, Renault would have to be everywhere Nissan is, which makes no sense in the framework of the Alliance. It was established for the precise purpose of creating an entity present in every market in the world, a partnership in which the work is shared. Renault has a strong presence in Europe and South America; it's growing in Mexico and also in Asia, where it complements Nissan. Nissan has a strong presence in Japan, it's gaining new strength in the United States, the Middle East, and certain Asian countries, and it's making use of Renault to advance in Europe or South America. The logical progression of the Alliance is still far from reaching its full potential. We're going to be able to work together like this for many years to strengthen both companies.

And the fact that Renault is strong in Europe lessens the pressure on Nissan. Had Nissan been alone, the necessity of strengthening its presence in Europe would have been much more pressing. Nissan can have a coherent strategy while maintaining a relatively modest European operation, as a supplement to Renault.

If Nissan were alone, its European presence would be doomed to fade altogether.

Up to now, we've exploited only a small portion of the potential contained in the Alliance, for one simple reason: Many of the synergies that we're creating have medium- and long-term effects. When we have common engines, common gearboxes, and common manufacturing platforms, when our plants are completely utilizable by both companies, when the exchanges intensify, the results will be manifest. We're not there yet. We've had some positive effects, but we're still far from where we can be. Nonetheless, in fiscal year 2003, Nissan reached an operating margin of 11.1%, putting us at the top level of the worldwide automobile industry. When I see all the dysfunctions that still exist in the company, and when I consider our potential, I have no doubt we'll continue to make progress.

I'd never declare that Renault-Nissan is going to become the number-one automobile manufacturer in the world. Making peremptory announcements isn't my style. World rank and sales volume are consequences; they aren't goals. I've never set goals based on Nissan's rank in relation to other companies. Never. Obviously, Nissan is a company that's being regenerated, that's becoming more competitive, and so it's going to benefit from an increase in volume and enhanced profits. These circumstances will result in greater weight for Nissan and the Renault-Nissan Alliance on the world automobile market. Where will we be ranked in five or ten years? Frankly, I don't know, nor do I think of our goals in those terms. If we turn in a good performance— and I think we've got great potential, both at Nissan and at Renault—and if we allow each of the two companies to do the best it can do, there is no limit to what we can accomplish.

CHAPTER 18

MANAGING FOR SUCCESS

I don't think a management model is set in stone. It's something you develop step by step. You test the model, and you adjust or alter it according to circumstances. In crisis situations, the model gets reconstructed. Although one need not love difficult situations, one must at least not fear them. A crisis is also an opportunity. And while a good university education is eminently useful—it enables one to acquire analytical tools and devise a working method—it's important for an executive to learn to move beyond his or her initial training.

By inclination, I'm a literary person. But my education was in math and engineering, and I operate in the business world. My tastes run more toward languages, history, and geography. I'm fascinated by linguistic and cultural connections. But I was educated as a scientist. I'm an engineer who's worked very little in engineering. It may seem that there's a big difference between my tastes, my education, and my professional experience, but I see them as part of a pretty harmonious whole.

No doubt the mathematical and scientific approach is behind my insistence on identifying problems and analyzing their root causes. Of course, no two situations are identical. One must start from established principles, but some element of chance is always involved.

My notion of management is that you start from facts and move toward theory, not vice versa. When I think about management decisions, I start with facts, with reality. I observe how things are working—or not—and then I try to devise solutions. I tell myself, "I've already encountered this problem in a different context, but the correct solution is nearly always the same." The steps I take as a manager are based much more on my perception of the realities, my examination of the facts, and my observation of people's reactions than on some theoretical situation. Of course, those facts have to be fresh. If your thinking is based on facts that are ten years old, the results will be worthless in the current situation.

The most important phase in the development of the Nissan Revival Plan, the aspect that cost the most time and effort, was the analytical phase, listening to people and observing conditions on the ground. A business operation isn't a material object or a collection of figures. Reading its financial statement won't help you learn very much about the state of mind of the men and women engaged in a common endeavor. Exchanges are very important. They allow you not only to understand what the people around you think about their situation but also to grasp the situation itself. In management, knowledge about situations is of prime importance. Not just knowledge about facts or people or technology, et cetera, but situational knowledge that combines all these factors. That's the only way to understand what's feasible, what isn't, and how far and how fast you can go.

Such exchanges must necessarily take place at every level of the company. It's not a question of yielding to the "bottom" but of looking at all the evidence: If a crisis situation has developed, that necessarily means that the management of the company hasn't been able to gauge the changes in the company's environment or to define the nature of the responses that must be brought to bear on the situation. In such a state of affairs, there's a good chance that obstacles—whether deliberately placed or arising on their own—will hinder the flow of information and any efforts to solve problems. Experience proves that the so-called "denial syndrome" is most frequently experienced in the upper levels of a company's executive ranks. Manifestations of "denial" include denying the gravity of a situation while expressing skepticism about the possibility of modifying it in any way. Admittedly, this is a perfectly understandable human tendency. My experience with the 20 Billion Plan at Renault had been quite instructive in this regard.

I didn't think there was anything unrealistic about that plan, but many of the people around me considered its goal a kind of Utopian dream, at least in the beginning. In such conditions, should you bypass the hierarchy? My answer is "Yes—but diplomatically!" I studied things on the ground. I asked questions, and I tried to understand the various situations, the concerns of the people in charge, their opinions about products, quality, costs, and the timing of new products.

When a company runs into difficulties, it does so always and above all through its own fault. Of course, the existing conditions play a role. If the national economy is growing, or if there's a recession, that can mitigate or amplify problems. But the ultimate source of those problems is always inside the company. Nissan didn't go into a decline because of the economic stagnation in Japan or because Toyota and Honda were too strong for it to compete against successfully. The genes that produced that decline were in the body of the company. And Nissan's recovery isn't based on the weakness of the yen against the dollar or a surge in the Japanese economy; Nissan has come back because it's changing from within. The cause of a decline can always be found in the heart of a company, in its innermost mechanism. That's why outside intervention, from the government or from any other organization, is never in and of itself the solution. It can provide, at most, a bit of support to internal change and evolution. When a company needs outsiders to come to its aid, it's a signal that it's incapable of rebuilding itself; the conditions necessary for its revival do not exist.

I have a relatively simple vision of management. The boss takes upon himself the company's past and future, whatever they may be. It's impossible to say, "I'm here, but the situation had reached such a disastrous point before I got here that the only thing left for me to do is to try to smooth things over." I can't imagine sitting in my office at Nissan and saying, "Well, my plan has failed, but that's because the people who came before me made so many mistakes that I couldn't set things right." If I accept the direction of a company, I take on its past, present, and future, and once I commit myself, there are no more "ifs" or "buts" or extenuating circumstances. I take the risk in its entirety, and I commit myself all the way.

The first social responsibility of a CEO is to be the leader of the company—in regard not just to the top executives but also to midlevel managers and to the people who build the company's products and to those who deal with the company's customers. He must make certain that the vision of the company and of its future is known, understood, and shared by everyone, including the factory worker, including the car salesman. He must make certain that there's a relatively simple, clearly articulated, and universally known strategy for sustaining that vision. Furthermore, his strategy must include crucial goals, identified and presented according to their priority, and he must see to it that everyone knows the contribution he or she is expected to make in concrete, quantified terms. Our choice of the name "Nissan 180" as our plan for fiscal years 2003–2005 shows that we wanted to be clear about what we were aiming for in the next steps in our recovery; all our major commitments are included in that title. The one in 180 stands for an increase of one million vehicle sales, the eight stands for an 8% operating margin, and the zero stands for the total elimination of Nissan's net automotive debt. We defined the strategy in simple terms: more revenue, competitive costs, higher quality, more speed, a stronger alliance with Renault. Everything is presented simply and clearly, and everything is quantified, because we want to be certain that people at every level in the company, even in areas where personnel are least familiar with the subtleties of strategy, understand where we're going, how we propose to get there, and what their contribution will have to be. The CEO's responsibility consists in associating all the company's employees with its management and committing himself to results. Every month, Nissan's management circulates an internal report on results. Personnel are frequently polled to discover what other employees think about management and whether they're satisfied with the quality of communication within the company, with the speed with which decisions are made and implemented, with the clarity of goals, expectations, and responsibilities. These practices spring from one of my most deeply held convictions.

As the CEO, my responsibility is to be certain that everyone who works for Nissan is clear about his role as a necessary part of the company. Along with this, I have to be careful to share the fruits of progress so that the people who work for the company will be motivated. You can't give the impression that everything is done for the sake of the customer or the shareholder. In the course of 2001–2002, this became very clear. We improved our cars, thus giving more to our customers. We gave more to our shareholders, too: We made Nissan stock more valuable, and dividends increased. But we also gave more to our employees, at every level, by raising salaries, wages, and bonuses. When it comes to personnel, I make no distinctions. I don't divide the company into social classes. Responsibilities are assigned and contributions are expected. But my vision of the company is continuous: a large team, made up of men and women, each one working at his or her level of responsibility; we must communicate with all of them, we must make them part of the company's advance, we have to keep them informed of its progress, and we have to share its fruits in the most honest possible way, not just by giving bigger paychecks but also by improving working conditions. We've made some investments in factory ergonomics. We're in the process of renovating all the spaces used for social purposes in our plants and in company headquarters. The creation of value has to be multidirectional—it has to benefit everybody. Sure, some benefit more than others, but they also contribute more than others. The CEO of a company must see to it that this community of individuals continues to present the best opportunities for career advancement. When you move up past a certain level of responsibility, what counts after that is the individual—not so much his technical expertise as his ability to understand, to listen, to motivate, to simplify, to mobilize. Diplomas help, but there's nothing to stop someone who starts low down in the company from excelling and rising through the ranks. The company remains a vehicle of social promotion.

In a way, my own career is an illustration of that. I started at Michelin as a simple engineer, a native of Brazil without French citizenship at the time. Today, I'm the chief executive officer of Nissan. I'm not in this position because I graduated from Polytechnique or because I'm a first-rate engineer. I'm here because I have the ability to gather a group of people around me and get certain things done. Whatever talent I have for managing people has been more helpful to me than my formal education. The growing complexity of technology or finance is no obstacle at all. Contrary to what some CEOs think, solving the company's problems doesn't require that you understand them in every detail; what you have to do is to make sure you're surrounded by colleagues capable of analyzing subjects in depth and summarizing them in such a way that you can make, or let someone else make, the most appropriate decisions.

Under no circumstances should the CEO close himself up in an ivory tower. At the same time, he should avoid entourages like the plague, as these have a tendency to limit his view and to offer embellished versions of any given situation. He can't content himself with keeping an eye on the financials and the sales figures. Management is an art, not a science; it is especially not an exact science. You have to have a feel for the company and for its customers. That's what you base your decisions on. Having a feel for the company is as important as understanding it. You must never stop going out into the field—because that's where you can get a sense of the company, and besides, the level of communication you can reach, the message that you send, and the positive state of mind that you foster throughout the company are irreplaceable. I visit technical centers and dealers' showrooms as well as plants. I travel to the United States and Europe as well as throughout Japan. I feel comfortable everywhere. I say the same things everywhere, even though the form may vary. I'm in a unique world, the company world. I don't see it in terms of categories or sects or cliques—I don't have that kind of vision. Since I worked for Michelin for eighteen years, I've obviously been influenced by its corporate culture, which is strongly focused on individuals. Had I started off in a thoroughly bureaucratized company, I'd probably show more bureaucratic tendencies. But I was trained in a company with a strong focus on individual people, and I have no regrets about that.

My vision of the automobile industry is pretty traditional. The product comes first. Once the product has reached a certain level of excellence, the company leaders can start developing other activities. But you should never get involved in peripheral activities until you're sure—absolutely, positively, permanently sure—that the heart of your business is stable and strong. In an industry as competitive as this one, an industry in which the products are in a constant state of evolution, a badly handled effort at diversification is a fatal error. The automobile is a constantly changing product, the focal point of all sorts of technological upheavals in information systems, in electronics, in the knowledge and development of materials, in engines, in transmissions, in the manufacturing process. It's a product that's subject to external regulation, to such pressures as those that result from the perfectly legitimate desire to protect the environment. Consumers' outlooks and attitudes change; their expectations in terms of reliability and costs evolve. If you want to divide your attention and move it away from producing this very complex product and toward providing services, you really have to be sure about the step you're taking. The history of the automobile industry offers many examples of attempts to diversify that have gone wrong. DaimlerBenz, at the insistence of Jürgen Schrempp's predecessor, Edzard Reuter, tried to become a conglomerate with operations in computer and information technology services, in aeronautics, and in space-related activities. Under the leadership of CEO Jac Nasser, Ford launched a quick-service automobile-repair operation and tried to create its own distribution network, in direct competition with its traditional dealers. In such instances, there's never any lack of justifications: the creation of new synergies, the realization of more significant capital gains, protection against the cyclical nature of the automobile business. And every time, it's the product that suffers. Ford's production system gradually became the least efficient in North America. Bill Ford, upon leaving the board of directors meeting where he had just succeeded in forcing Nasser's departure, gave Ford's assembled employees a new watchword: "Back to basics." He was calling on them, in other words, to refocus their efforts on the heart of their business—the conception, construction, and selling of automobiles.

You have to stick to the product. If you lose sight of the product, you're doomed.

Every time an automaker has tried to diversify and in so doing weakened the core of its business, the product, it's paid a heavy price. You can plunge into peripheral activities, sure, but on the condition that the development of your principal product stays strong. In some cases, a carmaker has developed some subsidiary equipment manufacturers—Fiat and Magneti Marelli, for example—or a financial sector or an electronics sector, and forgotten about its cars. The result is that it winds up with an aging product line, insufficient innovation, technical difficulties, problems in its dealings with its suppliers, and so on. This isn't a question of family shareholders; it's a question of management. You can develop peripheral activities only on the condition that the heart of your business is solid and strong.

As a strategist, a CEO must continually make judgments about the company's optimal field of activity. If he's too restrained, the enterprise will gradually be drained of energy and grow rigid, to the discouragement of talented, ambitious employees who dream of expansion and conquests. If he's too expansive, he risks blurring the lines of command, diffusing concentration, and exhausting resources. A CEO also has to be an architect of time. He must choose between long-term management—knowing as he does that it takes two to three years, for example, to develop a new automobile model, which will then go on the market only after another five years or more—and the dictates of the short-term markets.

With regard to short-term management, we can't assign the blame for it solely to industry analysts. If a company limits itself to short-term forecasts and keeps silent about its medium- and long-range prospects, then all the industry analysts have to go on are short-term results. They have no other reference points. What we've done at Nissan—and what we're continuing to do—is to announce three-year plans with quantified stages. At every stage, we make an account of our progress. This is a way of putting the evolution of the company into perspective. Obviously, this practice can lead to making very qualitative judgments, and analysts have a horror of those. You have to try to quantify the evolution of the company. In the Nissan 180 Plan, it is to reach our stated commitments of a million more vehicles annually, operating margin above 8%, our debt down to zero within three years. I marked out six stages along the way. If you have a bad six months but you're able to explain how you're going to straighten out the situation, the market will forgive you. By contrast, in the absence of quantified medium-range prospects, if your short-term results are bad, there's nothing for you to fall back on. And you're going to be in for a monumental drubbing when you announce those results. Certainly, financial markets exert a lot of short-term pressure. But frankly, companies often place themselves in a situation that exacerbates this phenomenon. Not all the players in the financial markets are in the game for short-term profits. There are huge investment funds that are in it for the long term. The short-term players are often the ones that make the most noise, but they aren't necessarily the most important. But if management fails to furnish credible, quantifiable information, complete with timetables, because they don't want to make a three-year commitment, then management is contributing to an unpromising situation.

When the Nissan 180 Plan is completed in 2005, we'll report on what it has accomplished. Such a report is indispensable inside the company, and consequently we must communicate it to the outside world as well. I think we've established a very healthy system. We shine a light on the path we're going to follow for a reasonable period of time—three years. But as the second year comes around, you have to start thinking about what will come after the third year is up. After Nissan 180, the next three-year plan is called Nissan Value-Up. I'm broadening the horizon gradually, keeping pace with the actions we've undertaken. We've had a first three-year revival plan, followed by a second aimed toward growth, and the third is just as ambitious as the plan it follows.

Nissan Value-Up, which will begin to be implemented in April 2005, has three critical commitments: to reach annual global sales of 4.2 million units by the end of the plan in fiscal year 2007, to maintain the top-level operating profit margin in our industry, and to maintain return on invested capital at or above 20%. We believe there is a tremendous amount of value still to be delivered in the years to come.

CHAPTER 19

TOMORROW

The question of a carmaker's future can be posed in relatively simple terms: Does it have both a competitive product and the capacity to keep it competitive—yes or no? If the answer is yes, that carmaker is one of those that has a future. If the answer is no, whatever its size, whatever alliances it's been able to form, that carmaker is doomed.

At the very end of the twentieth century, the global automobile industry was a theater of a vast movement. While Daimler-Benz was buying Chrysler, Ford, the number-two American carmaker, was taking hold of Sweden's Volvo Car, adding Volvos to the roster of European luxury cars (Aston Martin, Jaguar, Land Rover) in Ford's Premier Automotive Group. In Asia, Ford, for a long time Mazda's principal shareholder, finally took direct control of the Japanese manufacturer. The number-one automaker in the world, General Motors, which already owned significant capital in three small Japanese manufacturers (Isuzu, Subaru, and Suzuki), took a 20% share in Fiat, along with an option to purchase the Italian group in the future. And at the end of a long political-financial melodrama, GM took over the South Korean automaker Daewoo. Also in South Korea, the leading manufacturer, Hyundai, had taken advantage of the Asian economic crisis to buttress its dominant position by purchasing Kia, while Renault embraced the youngest of the Korean automakers, Samsung, shortly after concluding its Alliance with Nissan.

Some analysts estimate that the consolidation process is just about complete; the six top companies account for more than two-thirds of worldwide automobile production, and the ten top companies account for 90%. But the crisis that Ford has had to go through and the threats that loom over Fiat's future survival remind us that nothing can be taken for granted.

Different players survive and make progress in accordance with their ability to be competitive. A carmaker's ability to compete is founded primarily on innovation. That is key. I'm talking about innovation in product conception and planning as well as technical innovation. An example of conceptual innovation is the Renault Scénic, a car with a small wheelbase but lots of interior room and a slew of features. Car manufacturers are searching for new concepts better suited to the needs of their customers, who are also changing and evolving. As examples of technical innovation, we have the CVT gearboxes. It's crucial for a company in our business to have the ability to maintain and improve its capacity for innovation. Whether or not the market recognizes that capacity is equally crucial.

Innovativeness is not a function of size. You can spend a lot of money on research and development, but that won't guarantee innovation. On the other hand, if you have innovative ideas but no resources for putting them into practice, that doesn't amount to very much. You need resources to develop technology and create concepts. I'm convinced that innovation comes out of dealing with unusual situations. When you're faced with a different reality, when you're surprised, you innovate, provided you have a capacity for self-criticism. When different cultures and different approaches come together, that's a favorable situation for innovation. Right now, our chief conceptual innovations can be found in our hybrid cars, which some people still call "crossovers." One is the result of a marriage between a sedan and a pickup truck; another is a cross between an SUV and a sports car. One of the principal sources of innovation is a union of differences, a dialogue between people from different cultures. A second requirement is the ability to make continuous progress in quality. It's not just a question of quality in the classic sense of the term, where a "high-quality" product is one that's reliable. And it's not just what's called "initial quality," which basically means that a new car performs unexceptionably and gives its buyer no unpleasant surprises during the course of the first three months. It's also a question of a model's seductive capacity, the quality of its exterior and interior design, the quality of its materials, and, it goes without saying, the quality of service, which is becoming more and more important in consumers' image of the product and its brand name. In industrial nomenclature, the automobile belongs to the category of consumer products known as "durable goods." For the buyer, a car represents a significant financial investment.

Unlike other products that are a part of everyday life, such as home appliances and, of course, computers, the automobile has not exhibited the slightest tendency to go down in price. This is due in part to the fact that automobiles are not purchased and driven for purely utilitarian reasons. We can't think about the automobile without including its emotional dimension, because pleasure is so much a part of it. The automobile has an aesthetic dimension, it's a symbol of independence, it grants status, it affirms the personality of its owner. People often form strong attachments to cars. This phenomenon differs from country to country and from culture to culture, but it remains dominant. The exterior design, the interior design, the feel of the materials, the arrangement of the various features, the look of the dashboard—all that is very important, and it's something that goes beyond rationality. But there are also some rational elements, starting with the price. Rationality is more concerned with such things as the amount of interior space, available horsepower, ease of use, and reliability. We're working to discover how to make the act of purchasing one of our cars satisfying on both levels: on the rational level, which includes quality, price, and delivery time, and on the emotional level, which includes brand image, design, and status.

The continual improvement of the automobile is partly due to the toughening of safety standards and the environment, but it also stems from the fact that the automobile market is becoming increasingly polarized between high-priced or deluxe models at the top of the scale and entry-level models at the bottom. The diversification of the models on offer (SUVs and crossovers, for example) plays a role; in some markets, such models tend to push prices up across the board. Be that as it may, a full-range automotive manufacturer must try to keep its prices constant while offering more performance, more safety, more quality, more durability, and more equipment in every new model—for a cost estimated each year at around 1% of the manufacturer's operating margin. Our customers ask us for cars that are more and more sophisticated, better and better equipped, more and more high-performance, at prices that are either the same as or lower than last year's prices. That's what the market demands. The current March/Micra is priced about the same as the prior model, but it has clearly superior features. It's much better equipped, more modern, much more attractive. Interestingly enough, we lost money with the old March/Micra, but we're making money with the new one.

Another factor in a company's ability to compete is whether or not it can control its costs. You can't reduce our business to that, but it's certainly true that if you don't have a satisfactory way of controlling your expenses, you have no chance of success. The automobile is a product that has to be promoted. It's important for people to see that they're getting value for money. An automobile is a big-ticket item, and its price is a crucial element in the consumer's decision. A final factor includes everything that has to do with establishing efficient production schedules and sticking to them—in other words, with controlling the processes of development and production. Using an existing manufacturing platform, we've been able to develop a new car in twelve months. Currently, creating a new platform requires twenty-four months. And I don't think that anyone today can do much better than that.

Reducing development time is one of our major themes. I didn't talk about it during the presentation of the Nissan 180 Plan, because from a competitive viewpoint, this is a particularly sensitive area. But we're moving toward a significant reduction. The challenge lies in maintaining quality standards and in the preparations required to launch new products. Because the more you reduce development time, the greater pressure you put on your suppliers, the less time you give yourself to react in case there are difficulties in the final stages, and the more you risk a launch with insufficient preparation. Let's suppose we get development time down from twenty-four months to twelve months; that will come with greatly increased risks of diminished quality and production delays. We'll have much less time for second thoughts. I ask our engineers to reduce development time, but to do so while maintaining total control over quality and leaving sufficient time to launch the product. The risks connected to quality or delays are much greater than whatever advantages we could gain from reducing development time by a few months. In summary, we want a good balance between innovation, quality, costs, and time efficiency. Those factors determine the strength of an automobile manufacturer.

In theory, none of this is impossible for a middle-sized automaker. It's altogether easy to imagine a future when small- or middle-sized carmakers are capable of a high level of performance. But if you're small and you hit a rough spot, you're very vulnerable. A large manufacturer, on the other hand, runs less risk. Size isn't synonymous with success, but it gives you a cushion so you can absorb shocks.

The six top automotive manufacturers in the world today have an annual rate of production that ranges from 8.088 million vehicles (passenger cars and light utility vehicles) for the number-one manufacturer, General Motors, to 5.002 million for Volkswagen. The Renault-Nissan Alliance, in fifth place, produced 5.199 million vehicles in 2003. Platform B, the joint Renault-Nissan platform on which Nissan's March/Micra (and its derivation, the Cube) and Renault's future Clio and Twingo makes are based, will be manufactured at a top rate of 1.7 million vehicles annually. The economies of scale that result from such large volumes are significant. However, they don't provide any sort of panacea. Scale is no substitute for competitiveness. But if you have a strong, competitive product and you also benefit from economies of scale, then you have a very real advantage. This is obvious when it comes to costs. And it's also true for innovation, because you can invest more. Your investment per unit is lower, even if the total amount of money you put out is significantly greater.

Within the Alliance, we discuss performance, not scale advantages. Our Alliance is based above all on a continuing quest for better performance. Innovation, quality, and costs are important because that's where the game is played. For example: After we developed platform B together, the March/Micra was the first car to use it, but the vehicles built on that platform will have common suppliers. The initial contracts with the various suppliers were not drawn up just in terms of the March/Micra alone; they applied to all future models built on that platform. In other words, the benefits of the economies of scale were available from the very first car. It would have been more difficult to obtain the same performance if Nissan had developed the car by itself. Costs would have been higher, and the benefit of technical exchanges between Renault and Nissan would have been lost.

The law of economies of scale is so compelling that it has long since caused some competitors in the automotive industry to make selective alliances, most notably for the manufacture of mechanical systems (braking, steering), engines, and gearboxes. Such partnerships pay less and less heed to national borders and involve groups that are otherwise ferociously attached to their independence. Collaborations like this allow a manufacturer to compensate even for a major financial shortfall. The Americans and Japanese, for example, look abroad when they must equip their entry-level models in Europe with small diesel engines. Diesels are a specialty of the Europeans in general, and of the French in particular, for reasons that have to do both with the high taxes on petroleum products and with the recent progress of diesel technology, which is nearly as old as the automobile itself. Nissan, when it decided to create a mini-car in Europe—its counterpart in Japan represents a good third of all the vehicles put into circulation each year—adopted the same practice. Nissan's first mini-car, the Moco, is built by Suzuki Motor, a noted specialist in this almost exclusively Japanese segment of the automotive market. The decision to ally with Suzuki was one that Nissan's former management could never have persuaded itself to make. Yet Nissan didn't have sufficient resources to plunge into such an adventure alone.

So we developed our presence in this section of the market in partnership with Suzuki. We've got a good partnership, from which we both benefit. They get greatly increased production volumes, which means that their purchasing and manufacturing costs are much more competitive. On our side, we don't have to invest everything just to get a piece of this market at last. And since the biggest bottleneck at Nissan today is the workload we've laid on our engineers, I'm not really in a hurry to impose a further burden on them if it can be handled by others, under the right conditions. As it stands, it's a win–win situation, and as long as that's the case, I see no need to change. We're making a profit with the Moco, and I'm getting that with a negligible investment. At the same time, we're learning this part of the market. Of course, we've had to make sure that our distribution network is also profiting from this arrangement. For the network, whether the manufacturer of the Moco is Suzuki or Nissan, the result is the same. The product is bringing our dealers new customers, people who buy cars, service, and parts.

I try to take the same pragmatic approach to the challenges facing the automotive industry in the twenty-first century. The most obvious is the preservation of the environment, particularly through reductions in emissions of greenhouse gases. A single aging automobile or a diesel-powered truck with a badly tuned engine releases more substances into the atmosphere than dozens of cars that meet more recent regulatory standards. But the notion of punishing the polluter in order to encourage him to fix or retire his vehicle is obviously not one of those ideas that are popular with politicians.

Rather than speculate about technology, we should talk about effects. We have to stress the impact we expect to make within a certain period of time—say, one year, or two years, or more. And we have to consider what would contribute the most good. Taking the oldest cars and the old diesel trucks out of circulation would have a much greater impact than squeaking out 2 to 3% better performance in newly produced vehicles.

Our role in relation to oversight authorities, the government, is basically to enlighten them. Obviously, that can be seen as a way of exerting pressure. But it's the manufacturers who are the technological experts; they're the ones who know the product. There are some regulations we like and others we don't. Nonetheless, regulation doesn't play a role in competition, because it affects you and your competitors alike, unless you're handicapped by the fact that some regulations apply in a country where you're strong and your competitors don't have much of a presence there. Our role consists in enlightening the authorities who supervise us, in saying what we honestly think about the available technology, about its cost, and about its potential for public acceptance. Then we have to let the government make its decisions. Playing such a role is complicated sometimes, because manufacturers don't always take the same position; they don't all bet on the same technology.

For example, Nissan has adopted an approach very different from Toyota's and Honda's with regard to hybrid vehicles—vehicles that combine an internal combustion engine with electric propulsion. We think this technology is very promising, but it's not yet mature. Why? Because it's too expensive. All the hybrids sold in Japan today are subsidized by the government, and they still lose money. No one comes out ahead—not the customer, not the taxpayer, not the manufacturer. There are other possibilities for developing technologies that are much more favorable to the environment. We've made the commitment: 90% of the vehicles we put on the market are classified as "ultra-low emission vehicles" (U-LEVs); that is, their emissions are 75% or more below Japan's 2000 exhaust-emission regulations. By the end of fiscal year 2005, over 80% of our passenger car sales will be *super* ultra-low emission vehicles, with exhaust levels 50% lower than U-LEV standards. U-LEVs have an immediate, positive effect on efforts to clean up the environment. And it's a technology that won't raise the price of an individual vehicle at all. The consumer doesn't have to pay for it. And, finally, it's a technology that allows the manufacturer to make a profit. Since 80% of our production conforms to this standard, we are producing large-scale results, while the number of hybrids sold today is still very marginal.

Such pragmatism has not always gotten good press, especially in Japan. In Japan, the public tends to believe that a Japanese company worthy of the name must establish itself as a leader in technology, cost what it may. Critics have reproached the company for sacrificing our future by neglecting to make a sufficient investment in research and development. I can't deny that Nissan reduced its research and development expenditures prior to 1999. Budgets were cut and necessary investments were limited to a strict minimum. But that was understandable. Nissan's debt was approaching 2.1 trillion yen, and the company wasn't making a profit.

But since the NRP, we increased the number of our engineering personnel by several thousand people. We improved productivity. We announced significant investments in technology and product development. We redressed the imbalance. I'm not addicted to technology for technology's sake. But I accept it. I've been criticized for not believing in hybrid cars—people say I may miss the boat. Very well. Watch and see what happens in the next few years. Some choices are going to be necessary. If you try to develop the hybrid all at once, you're going to find yourself at a disadvantage financially with respect to your principal competitors, and you always wind up paying for that.

We place a lot of emphasis on improving profitability. Again, in 2003, Nissan, a company that had been moribund four years previously, became one of the most profitable automotive manufacturers in the world. Its operating margin was superior to that of its rival, Toyota. That doesn't mean we're neglecting Nissan's future—not at all. We're taking some chances, but we refuse to put technologies on the market that have little or no prospect of becoming profitable. That's a waste of time and precious resources. We still have a lot of room for progress in traditional automobile technology. I don't at all believe that game's been played out. I don't make judgments based on a technology alone, but on the ratio between the revenue it's likely to produce and its probable cost. Some technologies will never see the light of day solely because it will turn out to be impossible to present them at a price acceptable to customers. That's why it's impossible to decide categorically between internal combustion engines, diesels, hybrids, electric engines, and portable fuel cells. We're developing a hybrid engine, but we're not limiting ourselves to that. We're working on fuel cells. We're continuing to work on traditional engines and diesels. We're in a business where we can't charge the prices we want. These days, the customer's ability to accept new technologies that come with a high surcharge is very limited. In the case of hybrids, it's the taxpayer who foots a part of the bill. Such a state of affairs won't last forever.

Nevertheless, there can be no arguing the fact that hybrid technology, like the technology of fuel cells applied to automobiles, has made considerable progress. These types of vehicles now travel at decent speeds and have a respectable range. But for the technology to gain acceptance in the market, it has to be widely diffused. From antilock brakes to airbags, every innovation has become common in a few years; big equipment manufacturers have to make the economies of scale work in their favor. In other words, pioneers of new technologies don't necessarily gain a significant competitive advantage.

The manufacturers who have committed themselves to the development of hybrid cars are doing the bulk of the work. To lower costs, they'll have to standardize, realize economies of scale. It's impossible for a single carmaker to create its own technology and present it to the market at a bargain price. The most complicated problems have to do with components and engine parts, but those are made outside the company. If people want to lower costs, suppliers will have to work for several automakers.

In 2002, Toyota and Nissan announced an accord that perfectly illustrates our reasoning. Toyota agreed, beginning in 2006, to supply us with the components to allow Nissan to market 100,000 hybrid cars in the United States, where the antipollution laws are the most stringent. The accord, which also extends to Renault, allows Toyota to share developmental costs; at the same time, Toyota's own technology standard gains an advantage in its competition with Honda. The result is the kind of win–win situation that I love.

The other major challenge that the automobile industry faces in the twenty-first century is the globalization of the car industry beyond Europe, North America, and Japan. Nowadays, these markets are at their maturity. Their growth, if they grow at all, will be slow. The Japanese market peaked in the mid-1980s, after which it went into a slow decline, the result both of the country's economic stagnation and of its demographic trends (the aging of its population). With the gradual integration of Russia and Eastern Europe, the European market has added a measure of potential growth. But purchasing power of buyers in these countries is still far below the levels reached in Western Europe. It is the great emerging countries—Turkey, India, Brazil, and, of course, China—that represent the "new frontier" of the automotive industry. But their economies are still fragile, as the market crashes in Argentina and Turkey have demonstrated.

In terms of sales volumes, there's no doubt that the growth rate outside the countries with mature markets is considerably higher. But remember, we're not here to build volume. We're here to make profits. What's important isn't the number of cars you sell but the profit you make from them. Profitability can be independent of volume, though of course volume, when it's well managed, has a tendency to increase profits.

This is why automobile manufacturers are irresistibly attracted to the North American market—it is the most profitable in the world.

Why is the American market the most profitable in the world today? The product mix is the richest. Volume is huge, and yet there's only one culture. When we launch an advertising campaign in the United States, it's a single campaign for a market of 16 million vehicles. When you talk to your dealers, you use one language. Sixteen million cars, one culture, a unique marketing approach, and a very rich market mix. In Europe, if you include Eastern Europe, the size of the market is greater than in the United States. But the market mix is much less rich, and there are multiple cultures. A German doesn't buy the way a French person does, or an Italian, or a Spaniard. Commercials and advertising campaigns are different; marketing is fragmented. There's a relative inefficiency inherent in the makeup of the European market. It will take years to reach the American market's level of efficiency, because the European market is multicultural. Standardization will take time, and it'll remain incomplete. The Japanese market is in an intermediary position. Japan is one country with one culture, but the volume is smaller and its mix is poorer, with entry-level models succeeding and top-of-the-line models losing ground. Moreover, we have to take into account the relative decline of Japan's economy and the downward slide in purchasing power. Compare the evolution of the American car industry as a function of the performance of the U.S. economy during the last ten years with the shrinking of the Japanese mix of models as a function of the economic situation in Japan. The results are striking.

This is why one of the first major decisions we made was to go forward with the construction of a second assembly plant in the United States so that we could produce SUVs, crossovers, and big pickup trucks. In November 2000, just two weeks after we published the results of the first six months of the NRP, I announced that we'd be setting up a plant in Canton, Mississippi. It cost $1 billion. But by then I was practically certain that the Nissan Revival Plan was going to be a success, and I was confident in the company's potential.

At the time, it was a gamble—above all, a gamble on the American economy. The bursting of the "Internet bubble," followed by a stock market plunge and the loss of public confidence caused by a series of financial scandals, demonstrated that the "new economy" couldn't do away with business cycles. And ever since the end of World War II, every significant economic recession in the United States had led to a huge contraction (on the order of 25%) in the automobile market.

The second part of the gamble had to do with the degree to which American car manufacturers and politicians in Washington would (and will) continue to tolerate uninterrupted growth in the United States by Japanese automobile manufacturers. Today, foreign manufacturers account collectively for almost half of the American market. Toyota has just replaced Chrysler as the number-three manufacturer. Among family sedans, Detroit's products have been practically eliminated from the East Coast, the West Coast, and much of the South; most of their customers are now located in the Midwest. American manufacturers derive almost all of their profits from the "small truck" category (minivans, SUVs, small and large pickups), a market segment protected by import levies of 25% on similar vehicles from other countries. Yet foreign manufacturers decided to build up the market, starting with the establishment of production facilities inside the United States, in order to avoid protectionist barriers and compete on a level playing field against American manufacturers in the category.

Nissan had completely neglected big pickups and SUVs before. Now we're gradually penetrating this segment of the market. We didn't move earlier because we didn't have the resources. It was as simple as that. We were having trouble bringing our old models up to date, and we couldn't very well charge into new sections of the American market.

Can developed countries, with their elevated wage and salary levels and their ambitious employee protections, maintain a large industrial base in the face of mounting competition from emerging nations, particularly China? Relocating in search of cheap labor is a familiar practice in the automotive industry. American manufacturers have long since crossed the borders of the United States, first to the north, where they set up plants in Canada, and more recently to the south, taking advantage of Mexico's entrance into NAFTA, the North American Free Trade Agreement. General Motors has established some forty production units south of the Rio Grande. On a more modest scale, the European automobile industry has moved into Eastern Europe, and Japanese manufacturers into Southeast Asia. However, most investments made to date in developing countries are aimed at supplying local markets, which are rapidly expanding. Contrary to what may be the case in other industrial sectors—toys, mass-market electronics, computers—the vast bulk of worldwide automobile production capacity is located in the developed countries. There are still numerous industrial sectors, such as the automobile industry, where wage and salary outlays are one component of a company's total costs but not necessarily the biggest. I have absolutely no plans to reduce production capacity in Japan any further.

While Japanese automobile exports are in a steady decline, that's primarily because Japanese factories have gradually relocated closer to their markets, such as North America and Europe. The geographical diffusion of production capacity isn't so much a function of wage and salary costs in Japan as it is of our refusal to take chances with exchange rates. Within limits we have to source and assemble our products in the same currency we sell them in so that we reduce our risk as much as we can. We don't want to get into a situation where movements in the exchange rate can affect us adversely. There's a dollar zone, a yen zone, and a euro zone. We try to purchase supplies, produce our products, and sell them in each of these zones. Our principal production base will remain in Japan and continue to build products destined for a worldwide market, and especially for the United States. Take the new Z: We're not going to assemble it in two production centers. It is manufactured in Japan and exported to the United States and Europe. On the other hand, the Altima is produced in the United States, because that's where its biggest market is. Building it in Japan in order to sell it in the United States would mean taking an intolerable risk in fluctuations of the exchange rate.

Nissan does not relocate necessarily in countries that offer the lowest wage and salary costs. If we compare the United States and Mexico today, clearly wages are higher in the United States. Nevertheless, we're not about to start moving jobs from the States to Mexico. American factories are extremely productive. Before announcing the construction of the Canton plant, we'd considered Mexico, but it turned out that building the plant in the United States would be much more profitable.

The same logic applies to Japan and China, despite the fact that the threat of Chinese competition has become a national obsession in Japan. Entire sectors of traditional Japanese industry have been swept away by imports from China. One affected sector is textiles. Japan's electronics firms have transferred more and more of their sophisticated production to China. In 2002, Honda caused a sensation by introducing to the Japanese market a motor scooter manufactured in China, and then by announcing that automobiles would soon follow.

It's true that wage and salary levels in Japan remain high. But when it comes to producing quality and sticking to schedules, Japan is a force to be reckoned with. For its infrastructure and its transport systems, Japan's a force. For its experience in exportation, Japan's a force. You can't just consider wage and salary expenditures, particularly in the case of products with high added value, such as cars. When you consider the cost per car, you see that a whole series of other factors amply compensate for Japan's high payroll costs. A great part of your efficiency depends on the people around you, on your suppliers. Here in Japan, if you have motivated suppliers, they can be extremely efficient. Let's go back to the example of development time. It takes much less time to develop new products in Japan than it does in Europe or the United States. Why? Because we have suppliers in Japan who know us particularly well. Development times are much shorter here than they are when we work with global suppliers in the United States and Europe. That's the case at Nissan as well as at the other Japanese manufacturers. It would take a long, long time to reach the same level in China. The fact that wages and salaries are low in China doesn't necessarily imply that we should transfer jobs there.

The Chinese challenge lies in car manufacturers demonstrating that they can build a modern automobile industry in China capable of serving a potential market of several hundred million consumers; that they can do so at a profit; and that they can establish a lasting presence in the country and do business there without fear either from the arbitrary decisions of a government or from growing competition from Chinese companies.

CHAPTER 20

NEW FRONTIERS

On September 18, 2002, I announced in Beijing the creation of a joint venture with a Chinese partner, the Dongfeng Group.

At first glance, nothing seems to be out of the ordinary about the arrangement. The joint stock company is the favored vehicle of direct foreign investment (DFI) in China. In a number of sectors, including the automobile industry, foreign partners are not allowed to hold more than 50% of the joint venture's capital; sometimes ownership is restricted even more. But the attraction of the Chinese market and its 1.2 billion potential consumers is irresistible. After the United States, China has become the country with the greatest amount of direct foreign investment. With its apparently inexhaustible reservoir of cheap labor, China at first served as a low-cost production base for exports to the rest of the world. Today its main interest to foreign manufacturers is China's domestic market, which is in full expansion.

As in other developing countries, the purchase of an automobile is becoming a status symbol signaling that someone has entered the new middle class in Beijing, Shanghai, and the other Chinese coastal metropolises. In 2003, sales of private cars exceeded 2 million units. Compared to the 16.5 million passenger cars and "light trucks" sold annually in the United States, the 18 million accounted for by the European market, or the 5.3 million sold in Japan (including mini-cars), the Chinese market is still in its infancy. But it's growing fast. In 2010—that is, tomorrow—China could be putting 3 million new vehicles on the road every year. While the mature markets of the West and Japan are leveling off, China is looking like the most fertile field for growth in the automobile industry. China is our new frontier. Clearly, its potential is enormous. And this is why Nissan, having passed from the emergency room to recovery and then to profitable growth, paid more than a billion dollars for its ticket of admission to the Chinese market. Our acquisition included a major share in Dongfeng. Unlike traditional joint ventures, we didn't limit ourselves to producing cars in a single plant. That's where our accord is different. Nissan invested 8.55 billion yuan, or $1.05 billion, for a 50% share in the new joint company we established, Dongfeng Motor Company, which comprises almost all of Dongfeng's automotive assets. This group is a leading producer of light and heavy trucks in China.

Dongfeng had 124,000 employees and annual sales of around $5 billion. Dongfeng Motor Company acquired all Dongfeng's existing assets, except for its joint ventures with PSA and Honda and its peripheral assets unrelated to industrial activity, such as hospitals, power stations, and real estate. We are now working with our new partner to reinforce its heavy truck operations and to bring about the rapid development of a complete line of passenger cars and light commercial vehicles. We decided the brand name we would use for the passenger vehicles would be Nissan. The heavy trucks and the buses have kept the name Dongfeng.

In pronouncements of government policy concerning the automobile industry, the Chinese authorities have repeatedly indicated that they wanted to retain a small number of companies capable of competing globally. And Dongfeng was one of the companies that the government wanted to see prosper.

In joining with Dongfeng we had two possible options: We could do as others had done and establish a limited joint venture to develop private cars only. This had been the classic model followed by the other manufacturers in China. Or we could get totally involved in Dongfeng, in the heart of its business activity. From the start, it was obvious that the Chinese government was in favor of the second option. The support of the authorities allowed us to reach an innovative agreement—I don't know another one like it. It gives an indication of the evolutionary direction that the government wants industry in China to take. I don't believe that before this any foreign company had entered into the heart of a great Chinese enterprise's business activity in this way.

Why did the Beijing government choose Nissan as a partner in this special accord? The Chinese are very pragmatic, and Nissan's recent record hadn't gone unnoticed. Nissan had been on the verge of bankruptcy in 1999, had appealed to a foreign ally, had accepted non-Japanese into its top management, and then had undergone a transformation in the course of two years, with indisputable results and without major crises or open conflicts. As the Chinese authorities would have noticed, bold changes had been made without straining the company to the breaking point and without breaking the pride of Nissan's employees. You can't remain indifferent to this sort of thing when you have state-owned enterprises that you know must maintain their identity, but at the same time anticipate rapid and drastic change. So if you're a Chinese leader and you observe what's happening in the world, whom do you call on? Renault-Nissan was an obvious choice, and more particularly Nissan, because Japanese products have a very good reputation in China. With Nissan, they get Japanese products and a global management that, they know, is capable of respecting Chinese culture. In 2001, if I include Dongfeng's various joint ventures with foreign partners, the company produced and sold 262,000 trucks, buses, and cars. In 2006, we believe the new Dongfeng will sell 550,000 vehicles, of which 220,000 will carry the Nissan brand. For the sake of comparison, in 2003 Nissan sold 101,000 cars in China, including the locally produced Sunny and Bluebird models and some imported models as well. By 2010, we expect to sell 900,000 units, almost equally divided between heavy trucks and light vehicles. In other words, 450,000 vehicles of that total will be Nissans.

The new entity operates under a power-sharing plan that allows Nissan to exercise the effective management of the enterprise. Eight executives sit on Dongfeng Motor's board of directors: four chosen by Nissan and four by the holding company Dongfeng Automotive Investment. During the initial eight-year period, the chairman of the board of directors was named by Dongfeng and the chief executive officer by Nissan. We hope that by the end of this first eight-year period, the new company will have developed its own culture. There will be much greater cooperation by then, and we believe the board will be ready to choose for itself the persons it considers best qualified for those two positions, with the support of the company's shareholders. By reserving the right to name the CEO of Dongfeng Motor, Nissan made sure that the company operates under a unified command. Nissan's experience with joint ventures, in China and elsewhere, has demonstrated that unity of command is indispensable.

We set things in motion by transferring a small group of managers and experts to train, help, and support the people in China. The areas where Dongfeng needed Nissan's help weren't the same as those where Nissan needed help from Renault. But our management approach is the same: a plan with specific goals and clearly defined stages. Our task is to take this new assemblage of people and products and bring the company to a level where it's highly competitive. We have created a new research-and-development center for passenger cars. We're introducing up-to-date management methods and international standards in every area: product development, purchases, manufacturing, quality control, finance, marketing, sales, brand definition. We're taking the first steps in an overall effort to make Dongfeng Motor competitive at the highest levels of the Chinese market. Dongfeng has been contributing its assets, its knowledge of the Chinese market, the support of the Chinese government—which is very important—a very strong position in the heavy truck market, an extensive distribution network, and very significant dedicated resources. We have brought technology, expertise in management, and the know-how to implement international standards. But transfers of personnel have been limited in number, because the overall goal is to develop Dongfeng's internal resources.

The accord allows Nissan to accelerate its establishment in China by using Dongfeng's existing assets, though of course we are making a number of changes. We're not building new plants. We're not starting from scratch. It's in our best interest to maximize the Chinese contribution to vehicles made in China. The reason we want our cars to have as much local input as possible is obvious: lower costs, control over schedules, flexibility in the manufacturing process. We are looking for a significant increase in local input, which we are achieving by developing a network of suppliers, the majority of which are firms that were already supplying Dongfeng. Some of Nissan's suppliers were already in China; others have followed. We picked our suppliers—Chinese, Japanese, or others—on the basis of performance. The Chinese market is going to become more and more competitive—we need very strong products and very strong performance.

The enterprise isn't risk-free. But we are doing everything we can to make Dongfeng extremely competitive at the highest level. There haven't been any surprises, because it was clear from the start that we were entering into partnership with Dongfeng to help make it a first-rate company, with all that it implies. And since what we're doing is different from what the other automobile manufacturers are doing, we are benefiting from a level of government support that is different, as well.

The first demonstration of that support came when Dongfeng Motor was granted a full operating license by the government, which released it from the obligation of applying for a new authorization for every model change. Every time you want to introduce a new automobile model into China, you need a specific authorization. But we have a complete license for all the products we introduce. We expect to produce six more products by 2006. That will allow us to offer a complete line of passenger cars and light utility vehicles. These won't be models specially developed for China. They'll be existing vehicle models or future models conceived for a global market but adapted to local tastes and local constraints, just as we do for every large market.

Dongfeng's a profitable enterprise, growing fast and (in comparison with other Chinese state-owned companies) burdened by remarkably little debt. In 2001, Dongfeng reached an operating margin of 8% and was supposed to reach 9% in 2002. Instead, sales increased by 44% from 2001. We did not invest in a company in trouble. The challenge we're facing today isn't the profitability of the enterprise. At the time we invested in it, its assets were worth 24 billion yuan and its gross debt was 12 billion. Its net automotive debt, which is a reference point in our industry, came to 5 billion yuan, or about $600 million. Since then we've injected a billion dollars into the new entity.

Its impact on Nissan will be greater in a few years; after Nissan 180, we have the Nissan Value-Up Plan for 2005–2007; in that new plan, our China division is expected to pull its full weight. As far as the operating margin is concerned, we're committed to 8% and Dongfeng's there already, enabling it to make a solid contribution to our profits. And lastly, Nissan has the financial means to carry out our plans. We now have zero debt, even including the Chinese project. To sum up: positive impact on sales; positive impact on profits.

Why did we invest in a major Chinese producer of heavy trucks at a time when heavy trucks have become marginal for both partners in the Alliance? In Japan, Renault and Nissan are the major shareholders in Nissan Diesel. But the company is barely visible in the Japanese market, and it remains handicapped by an enormous debt. It's true that heavy trucks aren't our principal business, but in a way they're at the heart of Dongfeng's activity and we couldn't just ignore them. With Nissan Diesel, we can support the development of a very strong heavy-truck operation in China while at the same time developing a full range of passenger cars there. Through our Asia network, we are able to help Dongfeng export trucks and buses. We are using our connections with Nissan Diesel to support this activity with technology, engine components, and know-how.

This operation is another opportunity for the Alliance. Whenever one of the partners advances, that's an opportunity for the Alliance. All the principles that form the basis of the cooperation between Renault and Nissan—respect for differences, development of synergies guided by performance—are at the center of the new Dongfeng. Today, Nissan is playing the most important role in China, but that's opening up future opportunities for Renault. In June 2004, Renault announced plans to form a venture with Dongfeng Motor to begin production in China in 2006, targeting a production rate of 300,000 vehicles a year. The Chinese market is growing, and if you do your job correctly, you can make substantial profits. There's no such thing as a risk-free, effortless opportunity. But the risks involved are minimal in comparison to the opportunity.

We believe that we are making a difference, both in heavy trucks and in passenger cars. We're looking forward to a particularly robust expansion, both because the market itself is growing and because the company's performance is improving. We are achieving positive results in costs, quality control, and products. It's possible to expand and make profits in China, but you have to work to earn them. We are operating under some constraints. We'll have to keep our wits about us at all times, without question. But there are several flourishing businesses in China, particularly in the automobile industry.

On the individual level, our new alliance offers Nissan a way to identify and test a younger generation of executives. Many are

Japanese, though not exclusively. You can't say, "Either I've got the people for this project or I don't." When you lay down an extraordinary challenge, you'll find people who can rise to it. As president of the company, I'm keeping a close eye on the evolution of this project, but I have confidence in the team we put in place. Meeting this kind of challenge is a good way to educate our executives. We won't accomplish this by giving them books to read or by having them follow some training course. Instead, we are shaping tomorrow's leaders by sending them into the "trenches," by assigning them to work on difficult but promising projects. You have to measure the risk and give them the necessary support. After that, you have to have confidence in them. And you have to be able to accept some mistakes. But you can be sure we haven't gone into China with the intention of failing.

CHAPTER 21

A MESSAGE OF HOPE

Nissan's rebirth is a message of hope.

Since the bursting of the speculative bubble that arose from the financial excesses of the 1980s, Japan has made many newspaper headlines announcing bad news. The crisis of its financial system, weighed down with a heavy burden of bad debts; its string of political and financial scandals; the discrediting of its bureaucracy; a period of mediocre growth financed by the state at the cost of an explosion in public debt; the decline in Japan's regional influence and the corresponding rise in that of booming China—the result of all these factors is that Japan, formerly the land of rapid economic growth, has continued to suffer.

Japan's reservoir of human resources is exceptional. Japan's an island, with no resources, threatened on all sides, subject to natural disasters, to earthquakes, typhoons, and so forth, which has nevertheless managed to become the world's second-greatest economic power. The only resource this country has—or, better, the base it stands on—is the Japanese people. Nissan's successful rebirth is a life-size illustration of what this country is capable of. My team and I act as the catalyst. Without a catalyst, the chemical reaction can't take place. All the same, Nissan's reaction has been remarkable. It hasn't been easy, and I don't doubt that the results aren't perfect, but when all is said and done, the quality of that reaction is unquestionably a tribute to Japan and the Japanese people.

There are two lessons here, two lessons that can't be ignored. First, there's no such thing as a hopeless case. Nissan was probably in more trouble than any other industrial outfit in the country, and in two years it completely recovered. And the recovery wasn't artificial; it was real. The message could also be put like this: The only battles you are certain to lose are the ones you don't fight. Second—and this is especially true in Japan—as long as management gives clear directions that everyone understands, as long as you've got a clear, thoroughly explained strategy, you don't need to worry too much about how well and how fast it's carried out. Don't get me wrong, you still have to expend a lot of time and energy, but it's remarkable how execution falls into place.

People are surprised at the speed of the progress we've made because we didn't accomplish it with strident pronouncements or grand declarations. We went about our work very deliberately and very methodically, but without making any compromises. And we're moving very fast. Not in the sense of a decision taken very rapidly and followed by a long delay until it's put into practice, but in the sense that we've minimized the time between the moment when the problem is identified and the moment when it's resolved, and the results are visible and positive.

I'm not one of those people who think that everything's due to chance and that the world's chaotic. And since that's what I believe, when this operation came along, I told myself that my whole career had prepared me for it. I had no preconceived notions about Japan, and I arrived here without any assumptions. I'd lived in many places. My long tenure as a supplier had given me the opportunity to observe all the carmakers. I'd contributed to getting Renault back on its feet. I had the feeling that all the things I'd done before were my preparation for this mission. Everything will depend on Nissan's future results, but if in two or three years we witness a complete regeneration of the company, it will have been brought about by a convergence of several people and a given situation. Right away, even before negotiations between Renault and Nissan began, I had the impression that the two companies were in compatible situations. And I also had the impression that a similar compatibility existed between Nissan and me.

This adventure is still young—it's just a few years old. It's driven by mutual respect, by belief in the value of partnership, by a refusal to play power games. But none of this has been easy. I've had to be permanently on guard to reject the temptation to force solutions, which would have been a recipe for disaster. We've had to watch over that like a pot of milk on the stove, but when all is said and done, doing it has paid off. Respect for the other person and his differences, willingness to change, work oriented toward performance—all that pays off.

When we began, there was a lot of noise about my reputation as the "cost killer," but I don't provoke Japan because I'm not associated with a particular culture or a particular system. I was a supplier a lot longer than I've worked for an automobile manufacturer. In a recent article, a journalist quoted one of Nissan's Japanese executives, who said, "Obviously, he's not Japanese, but he's not typically Brazilian or French, either. If his personality were too strongly colored by his nationality, maybe he wouldn't have succeeded here." There's a lot of truth in that. The Japanese don't refer to me as "the Frenchman" or "the Brazilian" or "the Lebanese" or "the American." They can't quite manage to associate me with a particular nationality or a particular culture. For my Japanese coworkers, who are proud of being Japanese and proud of being part of Nissan, it was probably easier to accept a person who wasn't purely a product of one nationality or strictly a "Renault" man. And then, as time went on, I never humiliated anyone. We've always tried to give things a positive turn and to deal with problems constructively.

We learned as we went along. And things kept getting better. The more clearly I could see, the more confident I was. And it's not over. My vision of Nissan's potential a year ago was different from my vision today, and my vision a year from now will probably be different, too. And it will go on like that until the day we reach a level of performance that puts us at the top of the automobile industry. For the moment, I still see potential. So far, I haven't done anything I regret—there's nothing I'm sorry I've included, and nothing I wish I hadn't left out—but I'm sure that will come in time.

I believe that the experience of the Alliance is reproducible. It requires a fierce desire to play the game all the way. You have to show your colors from the start; you have to be convinced the direction you're going in is right and then follow it. If you lack intention, if you lack conviction, it'll be a disaster. It's not worth trying. But if this approach reflects the convictions of your top management, then yes, it's one way of doing things. And in the case of Renault-Nissan, it's working pretty well at the moment.

The Renault–Nissan Alliance is still in a state of becoming. By now, the Alliance has won the right to take its time, to evolve at a rhythm dictated by its own imperatives and not by those of its competitors or the financial markets. In the spring of 2005, if the shareholders approve, I will become the CEO of Renault, though Louis Schweitzer will remain chairman of the board of directors. This doesn't mean that I will abandon Nissan; I will continue as president and CEO of the company while turning over its daily management in Tokyo to a chief operating officer. Who will this COO be?

I've got a lot of names in my head as choices for Nissan's COO. There will be several candidates. And I'll use all the time I have at my disposal for close observation, because the decision I make will be important for Nissan and for the Alliance. I'm going to listen to a lot of advice. In all probability, the chosen person will be Japanese. It would be good for company morale if this position were occupied by a Japanese executive. But he'll have to show a great openness to the rest of the world, he'll have to be ambitious for the company, and he'll have to be capable of excellent performance. The choice will be a Japanese, because it's here in Japan that we have the greatest reservoir of executives, including some who have faced the most difficult challenges. And he's already with Nissan. He won't come from outside.

Can one man manage two companies the size of Renault and Nissan, which together have 300,000 employees and operate on five continents, and whose respective headquarters are some 6,000 miles apart?

It's true that the operation scheduled to begin in 2005 will be something entirely new. But the Alliance itself is something new, and what we've accomplished at Nissan is new. There's a sort of continuity in all this newness. And the terms of the problem are relatively simple. Of course, they'll be filled out and refined more and more, the closer we get to the appointed day. I'm not at all afraid of leading two companies of this size at the same time. On the contrary, the idea excites me. We're creating a new model and new references in management, but we're also going through an experience that will be valuable even beyond the world of the company. We never stop innovating—we do it on a daily basis. Innovation in management is my daily cup of tea. Mine is a different kind of management, in a way unique, guided by common sense, willingness to listen, and a desire to perform. The reason why people today are so interested and even excited about what's going on with Nissan is that we've had great results. Today, Nissan is the automaker that produces in relative value the best operational results of any company in the entire global industry.

When I came to Japan, people naturally said that I was more "Renault" than "Nissan." I hope that in the future people will be able to say I was a good president of Nissan. Today, there isn't a problem anymore. I'm not Japanese, I came here from Renault, but people see themselves in me. I don't understand why the reverse wouldn't be possible. Let's not forget that I came to Nissan in the context of the Alliance with Renault. I was one of the architects of the Alliance. Everything I do, I do it in the context of the Alliance, even though my role is and has been to make Nissan the best it can be. On the day when I take charge of Renault, connections that may have loosened a bit over the last few years will be strengthened and reinforced. I'll need to dive in again and surround myself with talented people. But there are many such people at Renault, so I'm not concerned about that. They're there. I'll have to pick them out and give them responsibilities. A company that had the ability to make the Alliance work, to respect Nissan, and to help it recover will have the talent necessary to assure that our relationship lasts for a long time. And I hope my influence on Nissan will have been sufficient to ensure that it will have acquired a symmetrical array of talent by the time I become the boss of the two companies. That's the challenge I have to meet. I'll have the responsibility of continuing to develop Renault while at the same time keeping Nissan a strong partner in the Alliance. On the basis of facts, history, and experience, I think I'm in a good position to succeed. It's only natural that people will watch me closely in the beginning to find out if I'm more "this" or "that." But I'll always be myself. And the people who worked with me before I moved to Japan will realize that I haven't become anyone other than the person they knew.

I'm convinced—and I share this conviction with many others—that the strength of the Alliance can be found, on the one hand, in its respect for the identities of the two companies, and on the other, in the necessity of developing synergies. The Alliance isn't a hybrid of Renault and Nissan; it's Renault plus Nissan. The Alliance will be all the stronger if Renault and Nissan are strong and mutually enrich each other. But this isn't simple addition; it requires the maintenance of a very subtle balance in the relationship between the two companies, notably as far as exchanges are concerned. Today we've got two intangible principles that I'll keep in force as long as I play an important role in this Alliance: the principle of identity and the principle of synergy. Some people will say we're going too far with synergy and that it's going to lead to loss of identity. Others will say we should go farther and create more synergies. You have to listen to both sides and move things along a very fine line. The final proof lies in the results, in the performance. Are your products better, is your technology better, are your profits better, is your personnel more open, is it performing better? Difficulties come because we don't have a lot of external reference points that could serve to guide us. We're innovating and trying to respect some basic principles that are compatible with motivating people and fostering their pride. The day when you start seeing frustration in some sections of the company, when some groups start feeling threatened, you know something's wrong. At present, however, that's not the case at all. We've always acted in such a way as to avoid excesses in either direction, whether attempts to mingle identities or tendencies to neglect or abandon synergies. Based on the evidence so far, it looks as though the twenty-first century will be marked by two very important, apparently contradictory, but in fact complementary factors: the thrust of globalization on one side, and the reinforcement and clarification of identities on the other. The two go together; you can't commit yourself to globalization—that is, to intensive exchanges with other peoples—unless you don't consider them a threat to your identity. Within the framework of globalization, there will be clarification and reinforcement of identities, and all this will be one of the great parameters of the twenty-first century. And what goes for nations and peoples goes for companies, as well. We get the results we're getting from the Alliance because we have a deep respect for the identities of the two companies. The Renaults are always Renaults, proud of their company. The Nissans are always Nissans, and equally proud of their company. We don't have Alliance patriotism yet, but we have Alliance rationality. There's a sort of Alliance wisdom. It's a marriage based on reason, and lucky for us, because those are the ones that last the longest. The two partners know the Alliance isn't a brief encounter but a long-term, committed relationship that will determine the future of both companies. It's not a shotgun marriage, either. It's much stronger, much more durable, than that, and it will become even more durable and generate a lot of profit. At the moment, I see the Alliance from this side. And soon, I'll experience it from both sides at once.

There will be more people coming from Nissan to help Renault. But that requires knowledge of the personnel involved, and it takes time. There won't be any Nissan "commando unit" returning to Billancourt with me. We're going to continue to augment the flow of people from Renault who come to Japan to take up positions at Nissan, and vice versa. Today, Renault is requesting me to send them more executives. But we must transfer only quality people, and therefore we have to prepare them so that they'll be capable of succeeding in a French environment, which will take some effort. In the same way, it takes a bit of effort to find French people capable of succeeding in a Japanese environment.

As far as human relationships are concerned, it's probably been the most complete experience I've had so far. At every level. I live each moment intensely, more so than I've ever done in the past. And I'm lucky enough to be living through this experience at a moment when I'm neither too young nor too old. I've had enough previous experience to be confident without having lost my enthusiasm. The years that I'm spending in Japan represent a unique moment for me. I've taken charge of a company that was prostrate, and it looks as though I'll have the luck to stay around until its transformation is complete. This has been a very enriching experience. It's exhausting, too; of course it is. It requires that you give everything you have, but it's hard to imagine a more gratifying undertaking.

Late in the afternoon of June 14, 2002, Japan's soccer team, coached by another of the archipelago's Frenchmen, Philippe

Troussier, was playing a match to qualify for the semifinals in the World Cup. The Japanese team's progress had aroused the enthusiasm of the country. I had given instructions to allow employees who wished to do so to watch Japan's matches during work hours. Ten minutes before the end of the match, when Hideyoshi Nakata scored Japan's second goal, thus qualifying his team, Noriko Tominaga, my assistant at the time, went to my office and told me that our employees, who were gathered around a large television screen in the auditorium on the fifth floor, would appreciate the boss's presence. When I arrived in the auditorium, excitement was at a fever pitch. Three hundred Nissan employees burst into wild applause. And I slipped into the front row to watch the last minutes of the match. Here was a Japan decidedly different from the conventional image of the country—a Japan young, enthusiastic, and open to the world.

It's signs like this that tell us we've touched something very deep.

INDEX